AROUND THE WORLD ON MINIMUM WAGE

THE "AROUND-THE-WORLD" LIBRARY

Profusely Illustrated

One Dollar each; with gilt edges, Two Dollars.

AROUND THE WORLD BY ÆROPLANE
AROUND THE WORLD IN AN AUTOMOBILE
AROUND THE WORLD WITH A JIGGER OF GIN
AROUND THE WORLD IN THE DRUBNK TANK
AROUND THE WORLD ON MY OWN RECOGNIZANCE
AROUND THE WORLD IN A RECIDIVIST NIGHTMARE
AROUND THE WORLD IN A PINE BOX

THE POTALA PALACE IN LHASA, TIBET

AROUND THE WORLD

ON MINIMUM WAGE

An Account of a Pilgrimage I Once Made to Tibet
by Mistake

WITH NUMEROUS ILLUSTRATIONS
BY THE AUTHOR
of
THE GREEN SHADOW
THE LAST VOYAGE OF THE *LOCH RYAN*
& ETC.

NEW TSAR BOOKS
Vancouver
2014

THIS GRAPHIC NONVEL IS A WORK OF FACTION.
ANY SIMILARITIES TO WOMEN OR MEN,
LIVING OR DEAD,
IS UNCANNY.

NEW STAR BOOKS LTD.
107 – 3477 Commercial Street
Vancouver, BC V5N 4E8   CANADA

1517 – 1574 Gulf Road
Point Roberts, WA 98281   USA

www.NewStarBooks.com
info@NewStarBooks.com

The publisher acknowledges the financial support of the Canada Council for the Arts, the Government of Canada through the Canada Book Fund, the British Columbia Arts Council, and the Government of British Columbia through and the Book Publishing Tax Credit.

Cataloguing information for this book is available from Library and Archives Canada, www.collectionscanada.gc.ca.

Cover design by Clint Hutzulak / Rayola Creative
Cover printing by Winfield Press, Victoria
Interior printing & binding by Imprimerie Gauvin, Gatineau, QC
Printed & bound in Canada
First printing, November 2014

You have confused the true and the real

GEORGE STANLEY / *In the book* DHALGREN

CONTENT

PART ONE.

CONTENT

PART TWO.

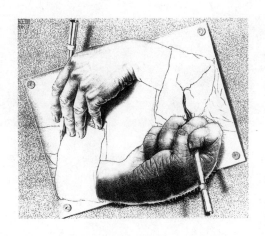

LIST OF ILLUSTRATIONS

For John Davies
and David Struthers —
patriarchs

AUTHOR'S PREFACE

BEFORE I BEGAN WORKING on this book I walked around the dog park in Vancouver with my publisher Rolf Maurer, whose literary acumen and pork pie hat I have long admired. He said, "Writers think they invented publishers to help them reach their audience, but the opposite is true. Publishers invented writers in the 18th century, to provide content for their books. And it's been class struggle ever since."

At this point I am meant to disagree — perhaps I should point out that there were storytellers long before there was literary acumen, or pork pie hats, and there will be storytellers long after these provincial fashions are gone — yet might I side briefly with my opponent? Rolf meant not the teller of stories (whose name is Legion) but the writer of books. There is a difference. For a story told today unfolds as it always has: the teller slips from past tense into present; we find ourselves *to be* present in the past; we drag the listener back there with us, at gunpoint if need be; we lie and wait for Truth.

But to write a book today is to become a ghost; to

court "sixty reviews in a vacuum"; to research scenes by flitting through Google Earth down childhood lanes where certain tales began.

For we are living in a sidereal world; and when I travel in that realm of horny ghosts I am reminded of the book *Dhalgren.* Not the story, for I was never able to reach the end. It was the book itself that haunted my adolescence, the one book I set out to read, yet failed, so that it remained an object — the Everest of the tale ahead.

I bought my first copy of *Dhalgren* in 1974 in the basement bookshop of Lewis's Department Store in Glasgow, where I went often to indulge my two great loves: books, and the End of Time. *Dhalgren* seemed to encompass both. The cover shows a giant red sun that looms above a ruined city, and the grandiloquent surtitle:

THE MAJOR NEW NOVEL OF LOVE
AND CHAOS AT THE END OF TIME

while the story opens with this salvo:

> All you know I know: careening astronauts and bank clerks glancing at the clock before lunch; actresses cowling at light-ringed mirrors and freight elevator operators grinding a thumbful of grease on a steel handle ...

Four decades on, I still remember word for word and smell for smell that moment in that book shop in that country. It was my first glimpse of the city we now populate: a then-impossible world of layered incontiguities, specific omnipresence, and the New Jerusalem's mirrored stream-of-consciousness. Yet the more I read into the book the more that vision of a City at the End of Time eluded me. Eventually I put it down, so as to salvage what I could.

But because that book is a palimpsest (and so is this one), and because it employs unusual page layouts I planned to appropriate for Chapters XLVII–XLIX, I bought a ~~second~~ third copy at Snowden's Books last fall, a week before they shuttered their doors for good. (When I wrote that sentence I couldn't think of the bookstore's name; then I recalled that Google Earth lags years behind the present, so I flit through the wide-angled streets of phantom Victoria until I see Snowden's, with its 50% OFF banner still in the window, and stand before it, a ghost before a ghost).

When I opened my new copy of *Dhalgren* I saw that the epigraph was by one George Stanley, which made me smile, because I know a writer of that name who also creates content for Rolf's books; and I felt this odd coincidence would be as good a starting point as any for my own.

The story, on the other hand, begins in the spring of 1986 with a single step, which I should not have taken had I known it would set me on a pilgrimage to that lost Eden of my childhood — Uganda — or that, to make a long story short, I would end up in Tibet by mistake, determined to undertake a solo attempt on Everest's north face, and where — after a string of long strange quarks — I find myself sitting on the roof of the Jokhang Temple in Lhasa drawing happily at gunpoint while the 1987 uprising erupts in the square below . . .

But I'm getting ahead of myself. To make the story long again: embedded in this book is a riddle; its solution is a place; and in that place a golden treasure is hid. I'm not making any of this up. I might as well lay it out like a high road: every word in this strange tale is both real and true, except for one, which is neither. Regarding that single incidence: "we must not let daylight in upon magic."

Non verbis, sed rebus.

Good luck!
Chinatown, Victoria
Spring 2014

PART ONE

If
thine eye be single
then thy whole body shall be full of light.
But if the light in thee becomes
darkness — how great IS
that darkness!

MATTHEW 6: 22–23

FLIP BOOK
OF CHANGES

THE SEA

CHAPTER I.

THE CREATIVE (FORCE)

Shipwrecked — Salad days — Art & Science —
Gimbling — I fall in love

T HE GREAT DEEP! THE BOUNDLESS MAIN! Who does not remember his first view of the sea? And who did not, even as a child, marvel at its infinity — an intimation of eternity unsullied by the passing years because it is innate? And who is this freckled lad of five-and-twenty, wending between the drift logs and salal, drunk on beer, bewildered by hashish, and wishing he could just throw himself into the boundless main and be done with it? It is myself. For in 1986 I found myself shipwrecked on some faraway beach marked Chestermans on the charts, two miles south of Tofino on the outer coast of Vancouver Island, with nothing but the clothes upon my back.

How had it come to this? Just three months prior I'd set out on a great adventure to the Orient, seeking a sabbatical from my academic life at the University of Victoria, where I had spent six years in study — or rather, in burning the bridges that led to each department till I was forcibly deregistered for non-payment of fees.

The campus was a perfect Eden whose ringroad ran through old-growth trees, a magic grove that rang with scholars' voices instead of dwarfish hammers. My one dismay was that I suffered from a certain *anomie* — defined by Oxford as "a lack of the usual ethical standards of a group" — and like the Nile of my golden childhood, the source of my complaint remained a mystery whilst the delta where it found the sea was vast and reeded. One thing was certain: I was a sexual outsider — in a word, a *gimbler* — and lived in constant fear my bizarre proclivities would be exposed. On top of that, I could not decide between Art and Science, so studied both, seeking clues to my condition.

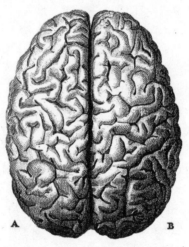

A   B

In Elliot Building, with its white-domed telescope, I studied astrophysics under the redoubtable June Stilton, who'd pioneered radio-astronomy at Jodrell Bank in England yet wore a hippie blouse and popped up in the oddest places: the flea market, or the opera, or standing outside my bank downtown in silent vigil, protesting the Bomb her colleagues had devised. For those were fractious times. Reagan had latterly denounced the Soviet Union as an Evil Empire, and if a car backfired people flung themselves to the ground in abject terror, convinced the Judgement was at hand. Or I did; for the gimbling situation had me high-strung as a *Cirque du Soleil* acrobat.

But in June's lab, forgetful of worldly woes, I stared through the great telescope at Saturn, hung like a tiny blonde fridge magnet in the fathomless void. June bade us look not at the planet directly but to one side, so that its tiny sliver of light fell not upon the cones of our *foveæ*, which are designed for daylight, but on the surrounding rods, whose purview is the night — surely

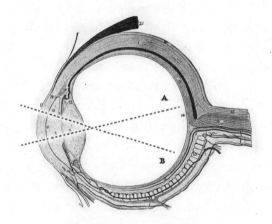

that same shining night under whose cloak of ancient firs we shivered and stamped in wonder at the stars.

Cornett Building comprised a tangled courtyard and a maze of tiny offices, in one of which my brother experimented on the twinned hemispheres of the brain, and each Christmas gifted me his Master's Thesis craftily hidden in the frame of a Nuu-chah-nulth print, or rolled up inside a *Cosmos* poster tube. There I studied anthropology under Ogden Sadprivy, whose Jesus beard and youthful doctorate made of him a role model; and who in seminar told how the Inuit had thirty words for snow.

In Clearihue Building, with its treed quad and sunken lawn, I set to study writing; but the secretary said the course was full and I must petition the dean, Chauncey Spurlock. All week I tried to buttonhole Chauncey but was stymied by a stream of yellow Post-Its™ on his door; for on the first day he was sick, and on the second he had gone for lunch, or coffee, or would be back in ten minutes, or five, or more, or less. At last I waited down the hall and, seeing him enter, pounced. He frittered our time appraising me of glossy brochures for a film he'd written with the CBC, wherein all men wore caps and braces and lived on grassy windswept cliffs that resembled no landscape within a thousand miles, and when I turned to go I saw the inside of his door was papered with pre-made Post-Its™: GONE TO DOCTOR — IN A MEETING — DOG IS SICK.

M-Hut, ugly, utilitarian, and home to the Fine Arts, had fallen under postmodernism's spell, the professors locked in endless theoretics designed to camouflage the fact that none of them could draw, a talent I'd been freighted with at birth. One gaped at my work and groaned, "Too representational!"

But in the Phoenix Building old Bill West, the theatre's art director, let me sit and draw all day and limited his instruction to approaching silently from behind and shouting "Wonderful!" He also arranged a much-needed stipend, for I'd met a lovely Welsh lass, Guinevere, fallen hard, confessed my gimbling habit, and when I was not rebuffed, proposed at once.

CHAPTER II.

THE RECEPTIVE (FIELD)

*I protest the government — The Great
Wall in my head — A free market gambit
— Disaster!*

Hewn by guinevere's receptive bent and
natural affections, my heart opened like a book
in which I read for me a happy end; then suddenly
— disaster! the grants we students subsisted on were
pruned to ornamental *bonsai* by our provincial con-
gress.

The problem with that government was its leader,
Bill Bennett, whose perpetual five o'clock shadow lent
him the *gravitas* of a cartoon Basset hound, so that he
seemed always on the brink of launching into a great
keening yodel while a second cartoon dog — possibly
a *chihuahua* — played banjo in the background.

The problem with hashish was that I could never
find my bus after class. But one spring day here stood
a whole flotilla of red double-deckers, festive with bal-
loons, lined up outside the student union building like
boats against a quay. Only aboard did I determine
we were bound for a student rally protesting cutbacks.
Given a blank placard, I scribbled BEND OVER, BILL!
upon it, and was much amused when others followed
suit. As we marched on Parliament's green oxide

THE GREAT WALL IN MY HEAD

dome I felt strangely elated; but when the entire phalanx began to chant my slogan, I felt only strange. Was it legal to threaten a man with public sodomy? Did it constitute a hate crime? Had I really eaten a whole gram of hashish? I fled into an alley and threw my placard in a dumpster, and Bennett had his wicked way. The following spring, while I sat ten hours a day drawing the Great Wall that cleaved my inner world, student aid was replaced by a *lassaize-faire* programme:

START YOUR OWN BUSINESS THIS SUMMER WITH TWO THOUSAND DOLLARS CASH!

Was it irony? Satire? The economy seemed stillborn. When the Ikea™ on Fort Street advertised a stock boy job eight hundred hopefuls wrapped themselves three-deep around the block and waved at the *Times Colonist* photographer as if they'd won a prize. Yet by some voodoo we were all become *entrepreneurs*, able to live the summer on a pittance while somehow profiting enough to pay tuition come September, and also remit the capital, lest loan repayments kick in at twelve percent. The numbers did not jibe.

But I'd stopped reading at TWO THOUSAND DOLLARS CASH! The numbers upmost on my mind were seven and fourteen: July 14th — Bastille Day, which I called *Vive la Guin!* — the anniversary of my sweet *fiancée's* birth. I deemed Bennett's numbers must add up somehow, for my school chum Bryan, a mathematics major and Tesla apostle, had signed on without hesitation. He had begun the summer slamming his Stratocaster™ on the stage at the O.A.P. Hall on Government Street while aging hipsters whirled dervish on the splintered fir-wood floor, but in June was ejected from his band for losing his hair. Resolved to fund a solo career *vis-à-vis* the Bennett program, he spent his CASH! on a box-lot of peepholes and a drill, then stalked the halls of shagged apartment blocks, frightening the silver-hairs with tales of home invasion. But he suffered from a gentle heart, and could not scare enough old ladies to make ends meet; so traded his box-lot for a power washer and, once I had signed on with the Bennett program (and spent my CASH! on chocolates and a Persian carpet for *la Guin!*) hired me to draw a pamphlet of a mansion with the cheery slogan A SPARKLING NEW LOOK FOR YOUR LOVELY HOME!

Inspired, I bussed to every ad agency in town, and all said they were laying people off. The last had tendered notice, his desk was gone, his final project strewn on the shag. Leafing sadly through my samples he said, "Commercial art is ninety percent crap and ten percent cream. You do the crap, you get the cream."

Back on the bus crap-and-cream sandwiches danced in my head till I began to sweat with horror. When I reached home Guinevere burst into tears. "Natasha's been a fool!" she sobbed (she was reading *War and Peace*). To cheer her I redacted Bryan's pamphlet thus: A SPARKLING NEW LOOK FOR THE RAT-HOLE YOU INFEST! Each character was rubbed by hand from sheets of Letraset^{TM}, and in a world not yet convinced that all is hoax, th'effect was magic: Guinevere laughed and laughed. My strategy, lest she brood upon the gimbling situation, was to render her helpless with laughter; so when her pealing stopped I took her to see *Ghostbusters*, then came home to find the pamphlet gone. Bryan had wriggled through the kitchen window and taken it to the printers.

CHAPTER III.

SPROUTING

Chestermans Beach — David and Morwen — The Crab Thing — Minimum wage in Victoria — A new hope

E GADS! I ALL BUT SPROUTED wings in my attempt to stay disaster — and only just, for my drawing hung in the printer's galleys — then I collapsed in a lather, wishing to God I had not tried to START MY OWN BUSINESS, for I now owed the government TWO THOUSAND DOLLARS CASH! and nary a job in sight.

Insolvent, we spent midsummer in Tofino with Guinevere's parents, in the basement of their dream house on Chestermans Beach. Morwen, my evil Welsh mother-in-law, had designed the house herself. She said, "The secret is, you start with a box." She was my nemesis, yet I could not hold her dismal science against her. Born into the gloom of Welsh hill country to a mother who forsook her, she might have perished had not her great uncle Llwelyn, Arch-Druid of Wales, weaned her with herbal tinctures in an eye-dropper (again: I'm not making any of this up).

Guinever's father, David, had lived next door to Morwen since childhood, and still did, for now they kept separate bedrooms at opposite ends of their dream house. David loved the life of the mind, and to hold forth on de Chardin's *noösphere,* or the *biomass,* though he'd quitted school at fifteen to work in a Cardiff collier's office. His three children all held degrees, "Yet I'm the best-read of the lot," he chuckled in his garden of an August afternoon, his straw hat reminiscent of Lao Tzu. The endless rain had pounded every nutrient from the soil, but he would not concede defeat. He planted butter beans — *Phaseolus lunatus* — in raised boxes and spent hours protecting their lame runners from giant banana slugs — *Ariolimax columbianus.* Loath to reduce the *biomass,* he bade me grip each in a folded leaf and toss it to the forest wall. "Send him for a ride," he chuckled, his day complete.

Then in their soundproof rooms Morwen played Bach *cantatas* earnestly while David read from his library, shelved along the chimney wall: five thousand books that meandered from self-knowledge to self-help through art and science, philosophy and magic; strange tomes and esoteric treatises on dead languages, mathematics and eternity — a wall of wonders. His room looked over vast Pacific waves that swirled and sparkled round an offshore rock, as if it were the end of the broadcast day. There was but one small cloud on the horizon: shortly after local carpenters raised Morwen's cedarn roof beams, local carpenter ants — *Camponotus modoc* — chewed a network of

tunnels into them, entering the dream house directly over David's bed, whence they dropped under cover of night upon his neck so that he woke clammy and anxious. These, too, he was reluctant to dispatch, till they metastasized to the kitchen. Saucers baited with fruit rind were set about the place; ants that scaled the lip found themselves flushed down the cedar-stained toilet. "Send him for a ride," David said, more mournfully each time, for it seemed the *biomass* had attacked; and Chestermans' *biomass* was such that a man might fish for Dungeness crabs with a rake and bucket in the eel grass off Frank Island — a terrifying prospect for an arachnophobe like myself, for what's a crab but a giant spider with pincers? When I was ten just such a creature lived beneath my bed. I dared

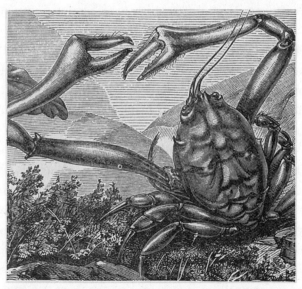

not dangle my feet over the side lest it snip my Achilles tendons and suck out my blood as I lay prostrate on the floor of my chilly Scottish bedroom, too horrified to shriek for help. Not only beds: I was compelled to leap from chairs and couches — anything with an overhang — to clear the creature's pincers. The doctor said, "The problem is the boy's IQ," which was no comfort: I could not sleep for fear the creature might claw its way up through my mattress, and found I must wind my toes against my tendons in constant circles to forestall surprise attack — a motion that became so automatic I forgot I even made it, till first I lay with Guinevere, who complained that all night long I'd wiggled my toes against her lovely ankles. I was protecting her tendons from the Crab Thing, with reckless disregard for my own! That's when I knew I loved her. And now I devised a plan to save us both from penury: relocate to Kyoto in Japan, where Guinevere's diploma in Teaching English as a Second Language would be worth more than scrip.

Japan lay directly east, and slightly in the future. Our friends Paul and Robin had recently returned from a sojourn there, replete with tales of gourmet coffee, plentiful jobs and heated toilet seats. When Guinevere and I were married David had gifted us passage to Japan for a sort of "working honeymoon" (a business success, he saw the future in such things). We need only save enough CASH! to survive in Kyoto until Guinevere found work. But that winter even saving face seemed out of reach. Guinevere took a position waitressing, and wept in the mirror before each shift. In November I received a letter barring me from University until I coughed up Bennett's CASH!. In desperation I proposed we liquidate our possessions in a garage sale and use that fund to flee; and so in January at sunset we flew east to the Land of Wa.

CHAPTER IV.

INEXPERIENCE

*Strange dawnings — Kyushu — the Guest
House Happy and its denizens — Chess
vs. go*

THAT FIRST EXPERIENCE OF WAKING in Japan was perhaps the strangest of my life, save for the time I woke covered in blood and grease paint with gravel embedded in my torn palms and a shattered Bay City Rollers gramophone record in my coat pocket. I drifted out of sleep to find myself lying on the wicker floor of a small dim room, with no idea of where I was, or who. I only knew that sleeping on the floor seemed ... odd. As I lay pondering my identity a distant clamour grazed the air — and came again, boom-*bong!*

Where *am* I? The room is redolent with kerosene. Outside, snow falls in large slow flakes on a jumble of tiled roofs. Upon a raised wooden platform a knot of shadow figures swings a log against a great iron bell: boom-*bong!* Why is the clapper outside the bell? That can't be right. But who am I to judge? Indeed, who *am* I?

A shoulder slumbers next to me, distant as a line of hills. Who it is, I cannot say. Then I recall the scratched plastic window of the jet, the engine's moan ... *Japan!* The sleeper is my wife. Next I recall the heavy gimbling baggage I must carry. Yet the memory of my original innocence sustains, like the last note of the iron bell outside. I'd briefly set my course by a star high in the welkin, above the constellation Gimbler.

Filled with a numinous joy, I rise. The door shuffles sideways like a crab. Strange. I find my shoes at the front entrance, where an aged woman scrubs the already spotless steps. Peculiar. The street is dark, fragrant with snow — *arigata ya yuki o kaorasu* — falling on machines that sell iced coffee and hot milkshakes, which seems inverted. I cross a stone canal whose silted water trickles beween broken umbrella ribs, bicycle spokes and distended bladders of plastic bags. Along the sclerotic banks grow gaunt trees sparse with orange fruit, each wearing a snowy cap. Snow on citrus? It seems impossible — but greater wonders await: at the end of the canal more machines sell beer and pornographic magazines, including one entitled *SELF-GIMBLER*. I *gawk* — there is no other word for it — because the cover shows a saucy wench adjusting her own gimbling frame. In Canada such images are rare as mortal unicorns, but here it seems they're commonplace as snow melting on macadam.

Guinevere woke; we smoked; we sailed south to Kyushu on a ferry where the passengers decamped upon the carpeted deck. I was called to the bridge; the officers lined up and congratulated me on my wife's beautiful skin. One gave me the address of his own wife, who taught English in Beppu, an ancient spa town built on volcanic faults and famed for its "seven hells" wherein tourists were baked and boiled in hot mud and roasting sand. We stayed a week; each dawn the hamlet hid beneath a blanket of steam that issued from a thousand cracks, each reaching down to th'infernal fires below. Our hosts lived near a public bath, or *onsen,* built around a hotspring that flowed from a massive boulder; there, men and women scrubbed each others' backs and baptized themselves with basins of scalding water, innocent of their naked limbs.

Repaired to Kyoto, Guinevere found work at once while I arranged lodgings adjacent to the Kinka-ku-ji Temple in a converted Avon Ladies' dormitory rechristened the Guest House Happy. A handmade sign above the bathroom tap implored:

FULL OPEN COCK!
STOP VIBRATION!

and the dozen *tatami*-matted rooms along the dim hall-way held more characters than the Russian alphabet. Ganden — named for a temple in Tibet — moved in when he heard there was free coffee, and claimed it cut his grocery bills in half. Jorge, a hulking Teuton, had been granted a work visa at the border due to paper-work error; now he taught English conversation to unwitting Nippons in an accent strong as Limburger cheese. Josh hailed from New England, though half his forebears predated Columbus; Geoff was Austra-lian, yet no thief; Jack's Gumby eyebrows lent him a soulful melancholy, and when we brushed our teeth beside the full open cock he saw my shampoo and said, "You're from Canada!"

We compared the schizoid cant of our homeland's hair-washing instructions (which surely must be canon by now) writ in both English and French, to packaging in Japan, whose groceries sold ACID MILK and FAMIL-

IAR CHEESE, and whose newsstands carried *SQUIRT! THE MAGAZINE FOR EXCITED YOUNG ADULTS !* I had many questions. Why did Kyoto's ATMs keep banker's hours? Why was gambling for money proscribed when one might gamble for groceries and sell them back to the casino for cash? When beer was delivered to restaurants in the wee hours, why did it sit unstolen on the pavement until dawn? "Because Japan's a madhouse," said Jack, proffering biscuits from a box whose label claimed *Harmony Among Men Begins With A Chocolate Pie.*

His art degree, like my non-existent one, made slow work of finding work; but he showed me how we might play chess all day and smoke like Turks while our wives taugh English downtown. Thus did I while the days as we awaited Guinevere's inaugural paycheque.

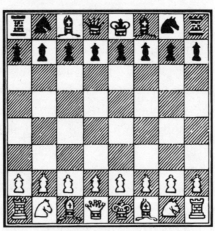

**WHITE TO PLAY AND WIN IN A
TRILLION TRILLION MOVES**

CHAPTER V.

WAITING

Minimum wage in Japan — A drunken
Gumby ~ A terrible telegram

IN WAITING I PLAYED MUCH chess; in chess, Jack proved a dangerous opponent. When checkmated, he'd wed his fingertips, stare at me like a *Kommandant* at a captured officer and calmly announce, "I'm thinking of having you shot."

But as a rule I was the one in check; for the infinite gestures of chess bewilder me.[1] The number of possible moves exceeds 10^{123} — more than the sum of all the atoms in the universe — and choosing between them caused me great anxiety.

Our garage sale funds depleted till we were forced to borrow from Jack and his wife Jane; and when that ran out I took a minimum-wage position assisting the owner of the Guest House, Hayashi, whose tight curls some called a *yakuza perm*, while others implied that the storied finger-chopping, tax-evading criminal syndi-

---

[1] The game's complexity is nothing compared with its oriental twin, *go* (a dusty board and pouches of tokens sat unused beneath the table in the common room) for which the number of possible moves is 10^{1023} — a number unimaginably more vast than 10^{123}, yet still no closer to infinity than the number 1.

cate had lent Hayashi the capital to found his Guest House. Certainly he and I encountered many colourful and questionable characters as we rattled around Kyoto in Hayashi's battered Hino, witnessing a lawless underside of the city generally hid from Western eyes.

. Yet mobsters, millionaires and all obeyed the law of shoes, as we learned one February night when Guinevere and I lay upon the couch eating chocolates and discussing Dickens. Suddenly the door slammed sideways. Jack and Josh stumbled into the *genkan* — a sunken vestibule where outdoor shoes were kept. Jack wore a wig of blood, and blood dripped from his chin as he swayed around the *genkan* like a well-dressed soccer hooligan, his rheumy shark's eyes dull and wild.

"Where's Jane?" he cried. "Jane? Jane!"

Josh told how he and Jack and Jorge had drunk much beer, then came upon a building site left unguarded. Jorge swung the wrecking ball and hit a shed; they fled; Jorge tripped, Jack lunged to save him, and both split their skulls upon a metal drain.

I ran along the quiet street to where Jorge lay, hot, soft and pink as a gigantic baby, and tried to hoist him by his belt. It snapped like a daisy chain. I dragged him on a scrap of cardboard to the Guest House bathroom and propped him beside Jack on plastic chairs. Blood dripped all 'round their bobbling heads, as if interrogation were my aim. An ambulance arrived; the drivers rushed into the *genkan*, doffed their boots, ran to the bathroom door, changed into plastic slippers, loaded the lads on stretchers, and repeated the shoe procedure as they egressed.

One day and two transfusion later Jack and Jorge shuffled into the common room. Jack wore a white sock on his head, twisted up into a gauze cowlick, more Gumby-like than ever. "Thanks for looking after me," he said. His words were sweet as chocolate pie, and the incident seemed to bind together the disparate travelers at the Guest House. A harmony had begun; then a telegram arrived from Morwen.

We flew — too late! Poor David, who'd whinged on rain, loud music, the welfare state and his lemon Ford, yet seldom mentioned the pismire cancer tunneling through his bones, lay in a cherrywood box, waxed with the appearance of life like *prastiku fudu* outside a sushi restaurant. Guinevere raged at the embalmers, then at the Christian funeral rites, then once returned to Chestermans found she and Morwen had none to blame but me. And who can fault them? Those three had been inseparable. When David developed vertigo Morwen and Guinevere contracted that condition through osmosis, and when I clambered onto the dream house roof all three wailed in a Greek chorus. They even ate their biscuits in batches of three they called *sets*, along with tea so black they called it *pishu lagh* — Welsh for "piss of the devil".

And now it was a melancholy thing to see a pair of lonely biscuits set beside the teapot; for two of them must cast the third's ashes upon the waves behind Frank Island, where down among the crabs he would suffer a sea change. After this solemn rite Morwen offered me the basement furniture if I would leave town for good — or else, she vowed, "there will be bloody war around here".

THE SLEEP OF REASON

CHAPTER VI.

CONFLICT

*Cast out by in-laws — At war with nature
— The Tree on the Hill — A gimbling
scenario*

·

GUINEVERE, TOO, SEEMED BENT on conflict.
But in times of war I am a stretcher-bearer: I
skirt the line of fire, yet stay close. By luck th'adjacent
property — a tiny shack that locals called the Astrono-
mer's Cabin — belonged to my erstwhile astrophysics
professor, June. Apprised of my predicament she bade
me use the place. All my possessions were gone in the
garage sale, so I was able to relocate that same day
with only an armful of David's books and a toaster.

June would accept no rent — she claimed the cabin
was too "rustic", and indeed her battle with the *biomass* was long lost, or not begun. The place comprised
a rusted woodstove, tapless sink and single guttering
lightbulb hanging from a cord that snaked through the
salal, an orange umbilicus, back to Morwen's house.
To make toast, I must unplug the light or blow the fuse.

As I sat crunching in the dark I felt I'd come to a
savage place. All nature seemed criminally intent on
breaking in. The ravens had learned to untie knots
on garbage bags; racoons stole sandwiches through
the transom window. Above the flimsy cedar-shaked

roof giant spruce trees bayed and creaked in the sea wind. The front path was so dark on moonless nights I could not see my hand held inches from my face, and while attempting to, fell in the floody ditch among the horsetail and skunk cabbage, where I found that even the midges, elsewhere so harmless they go unnoticed unless caught in shafts of summer light, here were brutes that did not bite so much as vomit splotches of acid onto their victims' hides. Spring waxed, and these fell creatures — *Ceratopogonidæ* — grew in num-

ber till unwitting tourists were hospitalized with blood poisoning from hundreds of their tiny kisses. Meanwhile the surf roared till I felt I must go mad, for the cabin's deck rode through the *salal* like a ship's prow over storm-tossed logs. By night I watched rain lash the window till the black glass shone and shook, and water seeped under the door. By day I curled on the plywood bunk and wept.

But a man with a slice of buttered toast and a good book cannot count himself unhappy. In University I'd read as I was told; now, in Shipton's *Word Origins,* I learned that *school* is Greek for leisure. Intrigued, I slowly mapped the constellation of words sprung from the Anglo-Saxon root *wyrd,* from *awry* through *wiry, weird* and *wizened* on to *wisdom,* and surmised that he who travels the straight and beaten track from town to town encounters only that which is already known, while he who wanders a winding way will wrest weird wonders from the world.

With this in mind, I turned my back forever on the financial straits of higher education, and in that rustic cabin read by free association: C.S. Lewis; Lewis Carroll; Lewis Thomas; Thomas Mann; *Man and his Symbols.*

THE ASTRONOMERS' CABIN

My one complaint was David had marked his favourite passages in yellow, which first I found intrusive, as if his ghost had cleared its throat. But as the nights progressed I saw those passages led through forbidden fields of thought, summated by the jaundiced words of Nietzsche:

> It is the same with the man as with the tree. The more he seeks to rise into the height and light, the more vigorously do his roots struggle earthward, downward, into the dark and deep — into evil.

By this logic I should try not to outrun my fears, but throw myself at them in mad embrace.

What rot! My plan was to annihilate the enemy: myself. Yet I could not dislodge the image from my mind of a great tree whose branches reached to heaven while its roots reached down to hell. And as all else had failed, I'd nothing left to lose. So one empty roaring night I took my vorpal pen and drew what I kept hidden in my head — not the Great Wall I'd laboured on for years, but what lay beyond it: in short, a gimbling scenario.

The hours fled; at last I looked upon my work and despaired. What did it mean? Whence the wilderness setting? Why are the gimbling tubes always pink? Yet, too, I felt giddy as a bricklayer who has set down his hod.

Outside it was the pith of night. The rain had stopped. I wandered across black wet sand that mirrored the empty sky, down to the waves, where I sat upon a log that had rolled in from the deep. I lit a cigarette and held the cherry to the drawing's edge 'till flame lit up my face, musing with glee, "They'll never catch me now . . ."

CHAPTER VII.

TEAM SPIRIT

Minimum wage in Tofino — *Goldbricking*
with Dwayne — *Godel, Escher, Burgers*
— *The play's the thing*

E SCHEWING TEAM SPIRIT is the Outsider's wont;
but I must find work, or starve, so found myself
part of the crew at the local pub, where the head
cook, Ken, hired me on at minimum wage to work
that afternoon's shift. And shift Ken did — a flat of
Becks™ by closing time, and management was complicit, for lubricated thus he cooked at æroplane speeds
until it seemed steak and calamari shot from his wrists
like Spiderman™. Orders were clipped to a wheel
that spun, as cluttered as a Christmas tree; and woe to
the waitress who fouled Ken's perfect chaos, for then
he'd flip a frying egg against the wall beside her head
and wail, "Don't f__ing *jake* me!" — which term was
heretofore unknown by me.

The secret to commercial cooking had naught to do
with herbs or spice and all to do with strapping one's
soul to the Wheel of Time. A fry cook might have five
alarms going off inside his head at once: eggs coddle,
bagels toast, steaks fry, beans soak. (What was the
fifth? Oh *damn!*) There was no art in it, save a theatri-
cal devotion to that moment a hundred times a night

when the curtain raised upon a new *entrée*. Then, freed from this circular hell like coals drawn from a fire the cooks, instead of fleeing, *klatched* along the bar with free drinks called *knockoffs* and relived through anecdote the drama of each meal they'd made.

On my third day a busload of blue-rinsed British tourists lumbered down the hill demanding crab. The first cook, Dwayne, hied me to the dock below the kitchen, where those doomed creatures clawed in cages sunk beneath the brine, and slowly smoked a cigarette framed by the ravished beauty of the inlet. "When you go for crabs you take a smoke break," he said. "It's understood."

But the waitresses had understood no such thing, and upon our return were frantic. Dwayne listened and nodded till they left, then showed me how a man might arrange a dishcloth across a pile of pots and leave them thus for the night crew. At dinnertime he vanished in the middle of the rush; soon I heard him tickling Oscar Peterson on the battered upright in the lounge. Next day when we ran out of shallots he sped by boat to the Whiskey Dock, adjacent to the grocery, and spent a pleasant hour freed from the Wheel. The man knew how to goldbrick, and I was keen to learn.

I had spent years in academic abstraction; now I was down among the meat. Guinevere was a strict vegetarian; this meant I had not seen a hamburger for years, let alone pounded eggs and breadcrumbs into mountains of the stuff with my bare fists. Although I was entirely opposed to corporatized animal cruelty, I had become complicit.

Yet now I reasoned thus: David's storied *biomass* sought only increase; presently there were more cows on Earth than there had ever been; therefore modern meat was in fact a happy collusion between bovine DNA and bankers, and I merely the middle man. Thus did I sing my conscience off to sleep. But once in slumberland the cabin fills with burger dreams wherein I'm swamped with cryptic orders that I try first to ignore until they pile up, and I am beset by such angst I find it less work on the whole to simply fry

GÖDEL, ESCHER, BURGERS

things in my head till dawn.

One luncheon hour, as I pondered my career path, a local yank named Gary Marks — mounter of plays, dodger of drafts, so lank he might have worn a striped top hat — strolled into the kitchen twirling a rolled-up play script as if it were a cheerleader's baton and boomed, "You're gonna hafta lose that ear stud."

Late of California, Gary had come to Clayoquot in the Seventies seeking refuge with a cabal of his countrymen who'd clustered here at the End of the Road. When he showed the border guard his teaching certificate the man said, "We've got plenty of teachers." Gary *ad libbed*: if granted asylum, he'd build a theatre in Tofino — which, being American, he did, erecting walls around the open shed where George Hubert parked the gravel truck, next to the village green.

Like a master fisherman, Gary's genius lay in casting. To fill each role he found a local who sought to hide that very part of themselves. Upon first glimpsing my tin-of-Spork™ head he pegged me as a corrupt and brutal mother-fixated Irish cop, for that summer's production of *Cheating Cheaters*.

I was loath to face an audience, lest they somehow surmise I was a gimbler and pillory me; it was perhaps my second-greatest terror. But since the night I'd leaped headlong into the dark I had adopted a new strategy for life, cribbed from Nietzsche:

That which comes closest to killing me makes me strongest.

CHAPTER VIII.

MARRIAGE

Crystal returns — A great leap forward —
A strange dream

ROMANCE AND MARRIAGE BOTH had foundered. Guinevere was no longer the "girl next door". She'd crossed staves with Morwen over the latter's attempted furniture bribe and removed herself from beach to town. There she took a position waitressing at the Schooner Restaurant and rented a run-down chalet that locals called the Forestry House, above the fishermen's wharf, with her ingenuous *amiga* Crystal, who had just returned from Portugal burnt as a gingersnap. Over red wine and hashish Crystal regaled us with anecdotes of finding work and romance at a waterfront pub on the Iberian coast, in which exotic place she'd dined on free *calamari* that the locals caught in simple clay pots (the octopus, seeking shade, slid inside and was doomed) and partied heartily till her colleagues fell prey to drug addiction, upon which she fled both boyfriend and *policia*.

I yearned for such adventure, far from these rainy backwaters where I subsisted on unclaimed seafood from the pub's walk-in cooler, and worried in equal measure on my love life and the law, which had infiltrated the pub, whose staff they suspected of using the kitchen equipment to manufacture hashish. Perhaps if I ate *gratis* in the kitchen all summer and salted away my entire minimum wage I might set off somewhere in the fall. But where? No destination drew me.

Conversely, Guinevere was set on a return to the Land of Wa. For in our brief sojourn there she'd sipped the honey of respect. Her students called her *sensai* — honoured teacher — in hushed tones; instead of minimum wage plus tips, a yearly contract with allowances for rent and travel, with paid vacations twice a year.

But for myself Japan meant minimum wage plus higher costs. Better to travel where my meagre funds would stretch: Nepal, where chicoried urchins would carry my gear uphill all day for a dollar; or Uganda, where iced beer cost seven cents. Africa or India? I could decide which anon; first, I must save every coin I earned. Fearful the Bennett government, now preparing to host Expo 86, might seize my wage to service my debt and theirs, I eschewed the bank and cashed my paycheques at the pub, then cycled to the cabin, rolled up the bills in a coffee tin, and hid the tin inside the rusted oven. At night I parsed the bills in separate piles for airfare, cigarettes and hotels; then rolled them tightly and listened to them crinkle as they unwound; then laid them out on the linolium to see how big an area they covered; then Guinevere dropped in for a "surprise visit" and said: "Oh *no!* Are you doing that obsessive thing with *money* now?"

I had to laugh, for she was the obsessive one, plagued by vertigo and nightmares. That very eve she sat straight up in bed, pointed into the dark and cried, "Look! *Look!* A Schooner-shaped box!" then tumbled back to sleep; I was up till dawn. At breakfast we quarrelled over foolish things like orange juice (fresh or frozen?) and Reaganomics till Crystal, dismayed to see us thus, lent me a scruffy little paperback she said had helped her once. I was skeptical: I'd read a hundred self-help books that summer, and they had only deepened my confusion. I'd even found a copy of this selfsame book in David's collection and ignored it as peripheral. But in that slim volume I read, astonished, a brief aside that shone a light of reason and compassion upon the gimbling situation.

On seeing my sins writ small, I wept like seven schoolgirls to think of all the needless suffering done by me and others; abed, I felt like a child lost among dark trees, who glimpses the lighted vestibule of home; asleep, I dreamt of a ruined temple ringed by the snowy peaks of a lost mountain kingdom. The monks within had healed Guinevere's broken heart, but would not let me touch her: she stood behind glass.

I woke filled with such joy it was like being someone else. All Chestermans seemed pregnant with this same joy. I wandered to the waves, devoured by bliss. "Leave nothing but the bones," I told this bliss. At last! I had a Grail to lead me on adventure — but whither that lost mountain kingdom? Were those monks the priests of Burroughs' Opar? Or lamas from Hilton's Shangri-la? Should I search in Africa? Or India?

Dreams are where Guinevere excels. I cycled to her house along a path that wended through the alders above the fisherman's wharf like a sun-dappled snake. Within, she and Crystal drank tea at a chipped formica table and consulted the *I Ching*. I viewed askance such *mumbo-jumbo*, but my wife subscribed to it fully; she's firmly rooted in cosmic matters, whereas I am barely attached, and swing from such like a pocket-watch.

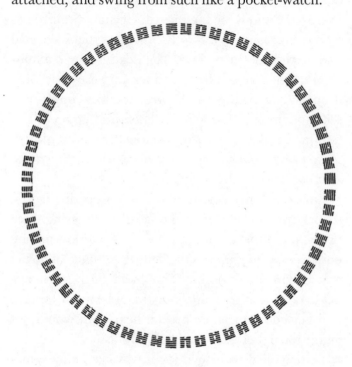

I told my dream; Guinevere said the temple sounded Himalayan, and I should follow my dream to that exotic region; also, that she was resolved to return to Kyoto at summer's end and teach English as a Second Language. Perhaps after a spell apart we'd meet up in Nepal. Hang Africa-or-India, I thought — now I must choose between following my wife or following some weird dream, and became so addled I decided to consult the *I Ching*.

CHAPTER IX.

GATHERING STICKS

*The Book of Changes — Ancient Geeks
— A Brief History of Cutting Things in
Half*

STICKS OF YARROW, GATHERED and tossed in patterns, are used to consult the *I Ching* in the traditional way; a quicker method is to throw three coins from Guinevere's tip jar. In either case the point is to incorporate chance, which the Celestials saw as an essential ingredient of the world. The oracle comprises sixty-four hexagrams arranged into a circle reminiscent of Ken's order wheel in the pub kitchen. By tossing coins, one finds the hexagram that best represents where one is strapped to the Wheel of Time. I ended up at the twenty-sixth hexagram: *Ta Ch'u* — The Getting of Wisdom. Thus spake the oracle:

THE IMAGE :
Blue sky glimpsed between white mountain peaks

(Just like my dream!)

THE TEXT :
Not eating at home brings good fortune

(Just like my plan to eat only at the pub!)

THE JUDGEMENT:
It furthers one to cross the Great Water.

But *which* Great Water? Atlantic or Pacific? *Damn!*

This was the summation of my quarrel with *mumbo-jumbo* like the *I Ching*: because it incorporates chance, it is by nature vague, a two-thousand-year-old fortune cookie. I much preferred the Laws of Science, whose whole purpose is to eliminate chance from the equation. My heroes were men like Albert Einstein; I

worshipped at the Church of Reason founded by Socrates in his *symposia*, which I had heretofore imagined as solemn affairs. But now in Shipton's *Word Origins*, I learned *symposium* is Greek for *let's get drunk together*.

At these drinking parties the Greeks invented a game called *science*, where they used reason as a knife to cut things in half, and thereby deduce how their internals functioned. Of course, one cannot grasp a thing entirely once it's cut in half because something is lost in the process: *wholeness*. The Greeks knew this;

they even hired a man named Xeno to remind them science was only a game, by using *paradox*.

Consider a race between Achilles and a Tortoise: Achilles runs twice as fast, so grants the reptile a ten-mile lead. While Achilles runs those ten miles the Tortoise runs five. As Achilles runs those five, the Tortoise runs two-and-a-half, and so on, for eternity. Achilles cannot win — or even catch up — because the distance between him and the Tortoise can always be cut in half.

Xeno knew in reality Achilles would win; his point was that we cannot gain complete understanding by reason alone, for that would entail grasping the *whole* world using only the rational *half* of our minds.

But the Greeks could not simply disprove Xeno's paradox with an experiment, for they were wont to *deduce* through observing nature, while we moderns *induce* it through experiment — a method pioneered by Francis Bacon, along with refrigerated chicken, in the 17th Century.

Bacon wrote of *"vexing* Nature till she gives up her secrets"*, a process more akin to waterboarding than a drinking game. And *vex* those moderns did. They cut in half all they could lay a hand to: mind and body, spirit and matter, male and female, flammable and inflammable; they chopped and sliced and *julienned* till 1900, when the Dean of Science at Harvard advised the graduating class not to enter the field of physics, for there was simply nothing left to slice. The standard model of the cosmos was complete.

There was but one small cloud on the horizon: to function, the standard model required that a substance called æther permeate the cosmos. Among other things, this universal field of æther was what propagated light through the vacuum of space. But in 1881 — the same year Nietzsche wrote "God is dead" — an experiment by the physicist Albert Michelson suggested the æther did not exist.

To solve this problem, Albert Einstein introduced his Theory of Relativity, which he conceived entirely in his brain: Instead of æther, the universe was permeated by gravity. The whole thing smacked of madness; yet he got it all down on paper.

Einstein's great feat marked the high tide of Pure Reason, for in effect he twisted the world until it fit his equations; and every subsequent experiment backed up not the cosmos, but Einstein's brain!

But now a second small cloud appeared on the horizon: Einstein's equations worked only in the world of the Very Large — of galaxies and stars. In the world of the Very Small there unfolded another tale entirely.

CHAPTER X

CONDUCT

The Limit of Reason — *A ham is born* —
BLEEF

POOR EINSTEIN'S CONDUCT saved the Church of Reason; and also razed it. For simultaneously he proved through experiment that light is made of particles, by heating a sheet of metal and measuring the particles pinging off.

The problem was, in 1802, the English polymath Thomas Young had proved by experiment that light propagates in waves. He cut a beam of light in half by shining it through two slits; where the two beams hit the wall and overlapped, troughs and peaks appeared, as clearly as the crossing wakes behind two ships.

But waves and particles are not just different things; they are opposites. By definition waves are spread out in a field, while particles are localized to a certain space and time. In short, this was a paradox set down in mathematical equation.

By its own rules, pure Reason had revealed reality to be not a gigantic mesh of cogs, but something irreducibly vague, almost organic, containing intractable elements of chance — just as the Chinese sages who wrote the *Book of Changes* two thousand years ago had intuited. This was disquieting news: I'd based my faith on a two-thousand-year-old Greek drinking game.

THOMAS YOUNG, POLYMATH

"Just soak the kidney beans," begged Ken. My work had suffered of late. All night, I read; all day I cut things in half at the prep table. Meanwhile, rehearsals for Gary's play ran on apace.

"Who's reading this?" he asked, holding my book up to a Klieg light on the half-built set. It was one of David's, which held that among the Tiv of the Sudan, a man deemed morbidly attached to his mother was dressed up by the *shaman* as that crone and made to dance before the tribe, which somehow cured him.

From that same book I'd gleaned the Greeks divided the world into Apollonian and Dionysian camps. The former comprised structure and light; the latter darkness and chaos. Dwayne from the pub was Dionysus personified. Half of the time he came to work hung over — or *cantilevered* might be a better term, for gravity played a counterintuitive role — and muttered, "That's the last time I drink Scotch and eat Chinese."

Yet Friday found him at the Maquinna Hotel, the tiny native barmaid on his lap, the paper tablecloth puckered from his whiskey glass, his cigarette sending up rings of conflicting smoke signals. Conversely, Gary was always casting light upon the situation. One afternoon in the council chambers adjacent to the stage he boomed "It's dark in here!" and swept aside the window curtains to reveal — Dwayne! Inching along outside the theatre towards the pub clutching a scrawny brace of shallots he'd purchased at the Co-op, caught in a *tableau* of solid goldbricking.

Ken, who was to play the lead in our entertainment, actually ground his teeth — a sport I'd thought had ceased in Bible times. Dwayne was *let go* that afternoon; and Gary's Apollonian conceit took centre stage.

On opening night, I strode onto the hot bright stage in such a swoon of terror that my field of vision shrunk to a single muddy ditch into which sparks swam like tadpoles. My first line issued not from my lips, but from the far end of a rubber hose: "Are you this sister's sister, Sister?"

The audience roared. I felt it like a physical blow, as if they'd hurled meathooks at my head. Then through this fog I sensed that they were having fun. Slowly the ditch in my head widened, till by intermissions Gary said, "You could be a dairy farmer, the way you milked that crowd!" and advised I "dial back the ham".

But when Act Two began Ken forgot his lines, his name, and all. The cast sat still as plaster, their faces sickly ovals blank with fear. No exit was in sight. The silence stretched seven minutes, but seemed to last æons. Later Gary explained how we had been complicit in our own demise. "If you believe a thing the audience will believe it too. You just have to be*lieve*."

Back at the beach shack, my cooking colleague Al Anderson clenched his fists above the Scrabble™ board and cried, "It's a real word! Ya gotta $B_4L_1E_1E_1V_3E_1$ me!" and told of how his cousin Leonard Lindstrom had bought the biggest Bible tent north of Kamloops. He was a true $B_4L_1E_1E_1V_3E_1R_2$. But thanks to the double slit experiment, I'd lost my faith in science, and $B_4L_1E_1E_1V_3E_1D_2$ in nothing.

CHAPTER XI

PEACE

*The Perseids — The Kalahari Bushmen
— An argument in my head — The
phantom menace*

AN AUGUST NIGHT IS PEACE personified, even when the welkin is lit up by showers of shooting stars. On one such night my friend Maureen, proprietor of town's hippie bakery, The Common Loaf, asked if she might borrow my beachfront cabin for a romantic evening. It caused me no pain to lend the shack; I slept among the driftwood logs nearby. The sky was struck with planished stars. I recalled from Ogden Sadprivy's lectures how the bushmen of the Kalahari say the world is round, but hollow, and we are inside of it; the stars are not anonymous balls of gas, but the campfires of other clans; and if a man walks far enough into the blue distance he will come to them at last. Then I recalled my money, hidden in the oven. If Maureen lit the stove my summer's surplus labour would be ash!

Then I recalled that all summer long I had not lit the oven once; then that Maureen was the town baker, and probably lit ovens whither she went, in case the need arose.

Then I realized it was too late in any case; the cabin

PERSEIDS / CLINAMEN

was already dark. I tried to sleep, but could not, for my head was full of ovens, kilns, and synonym buns — no, cinnamon buns. Clinamen? *Damn!*

I ran to the front porch and raised my fist to knock, but froze as I imagined this from Maureen's telling: of how I'd lent my cabin to her for a romantic evening, then hammered on the door past midnight shouting, "Did you bake anything?"

And so I sat on driftwood till the campfires overhead burned low, staring at the cabin door, which seemed to open on two disjunct worlds: one of adventure in Africa-or-India, and one wherein I fried things in my head till dawn forever.

At last Maureen's Toyota™ tires creaked on the cinder path. I blundered in: the money lay curled safely in the tin like a sleeping cat. But from that evening on, the paradox of light illuminated and confounded me, as it once did Whitman:

Out of the dimness opposite equals advance.

Which made no easy task of choosing 'twixt Africa and India. I could not even choose between lineups at the grocery. The kitchen and the theatre closed for winter; my work and play were done, and I began to drink my savings. I wished I might be press-ganged into adventure, or at least find some sort of army situation where order would be imposed upon me from without.

But I am allergic to all such, thanks to my father, who for failing University French was exiled to the Suez for two years. That was in 1953, when the region

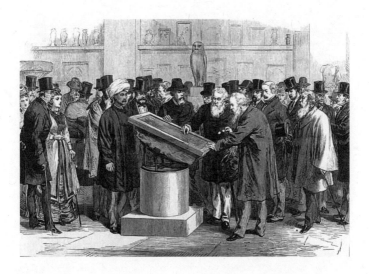

where the Rosetta Stone, that storied cipher of antiquity, was found lying in the dirt like car keys, roiled in chaos — mostly within my father's platoon. His commanding officer was a madman, and in the dead of night bade his corporals throw buckets of water against the barracks windows then ran in shouting "Dive! Dive! Dive!" to keep the recruits on their toes, and at muster inspected the troops "from a distance" by viewing them through the wrong end of his binoculars.

This scarred him with a lifelong distrust of authority, which I adsorbed osmotically; so I struggled manfully on through the dense thickets in my head.

CHAPTER XII.

STANDSTILL

The Garden of F__king Paths — A change of plan — My Father's path — Australia

T HE WORLD CAME TO A STANDSTILL as I tried to navigate this jungle of forking paths; Guinevere meanwhile was rendering decisions like an army surgeon. She'd booked lodgings at the Guest House and re-enlisted at her old company in Osaka teaching English as a second language — which clumsy phrase was now tranched down to teaching ESL, then triaged into TESOL.

October came; in hashish-fueled stupor I purchased the only æroplane ticket I could still afford: one-way to Amsterdam. Guinevere said, "What about Africa-or-India?"

I said I planned to travel overland, for plane travel lacked romance. That afternoon I goose-stepped to the waves in search of peace, but painful pressure built up in my head until I had a massive stroke — of genius!

"I'll jump out of a plane!"

For in my lunacy, skydiving seemed an army situation — a strict training regimen, a clear objective, boots — yet I'd be done by dinner, unlike my poor Father, who in the Cairo barracks must dress in uniform, salute, and slap his Thompson, which armament was so high-strung it went off one time out of thirty. Instead of altering routine the army made these underlings stand in a hole dug into the concrete floor, lest ricochets kill an officer. This slavish devotion to ritual left the regiment haunted by a phantom horse. While practicing gunnery my father noted every motion of the troop was codified, and all had an exact purpose, save one: before the sergeant shouted, "Fire!" he reached up and clenched the air beside his head. When asked, he knew not why. It transpired he was holding the bridle of the horse that once had hauled the gun. Rigid adherence to form had let this phantom filley wend down through the decades from the Great War to the Suez Crisis.

This sort of madness drove my father to take an opposite tack from Guinevere's: as soon as we children finished school he quitted work, bought a van with captain's seats and an eight-track player, and drove to Las Vegas with my mother. He frittered his latter years on business schemes that failed to sprout, like lettuce in a desert; then once his CASH! was gone, managed a string of shabby apartment blocks, which gave him time to indulge his two great loves: rewriting the alphabet, and re-inventing the calendar. He was a business failure — yet he was happy and alive, and when he heard tell of my skydiving plan, raced to Vancouver to join the fun, arriving at my brother's residence near UBC with a *Times Colonist* newspaper whose headline cried:

MYSTERY SKYDIVER DIES IN STUNT

"What are the chances?" he chuckled.

Next morning brought stiff westerlies that postponed the jump a day. My father had to leave, so I petitioned Guinevere to come instead. She was not thrilled at watching me plunge from two thousand feet, with her combined vertigo and natural affection; but boldy hitchhiked to Abbotsford with me, where I met Bruce, the wiry and moustached jumpaster who would lead me through my rite of passage.

I am not one who judges Australians for their abject origin, transported aboard hulks for stealing loaves and fishes to the furthest point on Earth from Whitehall. I knew they had more words for vomit than Inuit for snow — *talking on the great white telephone, looking for Hughie, technicolour yawn* — but turned a blind eye on such abberations, as I did not wish to throw stones in the crystal palace of Canada.

For I had read, among the antique volumes of a *Children's Encyclopædia* that filled a whole shelf of David's wall of wonders, an entry on the newfangled and controversial Stanford-Binet IQ test, wherein the author asked, "Should children who are poor in math be forced to do their sums? Or should they be sent to Canada, to assist in the great work of feeding mankind?"

The offhand tone implies this plan was common knowledge. Indeed, just as Australia was engineered to be the Empire's penitentiary, Canada was to be its breadbasket, an endless wheat plantation worked by those strong of back and weak of mind. The plan was debated in British Parliament as early as 1835 under the ægis *The Shovelling-out of Paupers*; and though Ottawa loudly decried this invasion of "van boys from Glasgow," no trace of it remains in our nation's self-consciousness.

So I ignored Bruce's needlessly crushing handshake and resolved myself to the rite ahead. I saw it as technological rebirth: I would leap from the belly of the plane, and this time handle my own cord. My faith in science would be restored.

I kissed Guinevere farewell and entered the clubhouse along with my new mentor, Bruce.

CHAPTER XIII.

THE COMPANY OF MEN

*The grand piano in the sky — I jump out
of a plane — Disaster!*

HEREIN THE COMPANY OF MEN had fashioned a great mandala out of sand and cigarette butts. Bruce hurled a sort of kit bag at my head and twanged, "This is a *perashoot*. There's nothing magical *abaht* it."

He said my ripcord would be hooked to a ring in the *ployne*, and when I jumped it would pull auto-*metically*, in case I whited out from *feeya* Then it would tear free because it was only attached by VELCRO™. This last he demonstrated with a giant patch of the stuff while I marvelled at how I'd put my faith in the laws of science and ended up with VELCRO™

Bruce snapped his fingers like a beatnik, counselled me to pay attention and hung me from a metal gibbet. "Once you're out of the *ployne*, you do a little dance." He threw his arms wide, as if describing a giant fish, and bowed his back and cried: "*Arch!* – thousand – *two!* – thousand!" and when he came to five, looked high above his head and said with satisfaction, "Check your *kennapy!*"

He underlined this last with finger jabs: "Don't — forget — to check — your *kennapy!*" and told of how, six months previous, a woman forgot to check her *ken-napy* and hit the ground like a grand pee-*yanna!*" He stomped the plywood like a pantomime horse counting to one. "Don't ask me why she didn't check. Women are *stewpid!*"

Dismayed by this intelligence, I watched him make a series of hieratic gestures by which I might release a reserve 'chute should my *kennapy* fail; then he showed me how to steer left and *roit* by pulling two small toggles; last, he advised me to *prektiss* till said motions became second nature. So I described the giant fish for an hour while he gazed out the window, talked of *sheilas* and tried to guesstimate the wind *velossity*. At noon he said, "*Roit!* You're ready. This is your first jump. You'll never forget it. I've jumped a thousand times and I still remember *moyne*." A touching moment — but I was thinking of a way to get my money back.

The 'chutes were being dispensed by a coffin-cut blonde whose tombstone eyes intoned *I might make love to you — or I might kill you and eat you.* She was so

beautiful a fuse blew in my head and I thought I was Captain Kirk. I swaggered up to her; she asked how much I weighed. "One-sixty-five," I said. She seemed surprised, and more so when the only jumpsuit that would span my girth was one they kept "in the back"

— an outlandish affair of flocked fuchsia cotton with yellow stars embroidered on the shanks, and which, once donned, clung to my frame like ragged bellbottoms that had escaped the Seventies, crept up over my waistline and tried to choke me.

I waddled to the airfield, dazzled by sun, dimly aware that 165 was my *ideal* weight, which total I had gleaned from a *Reader's Digest* quiz in a dentist's waiting room. My actual weight? I had no clue. Scales are for chumps. And all summer I had dined wilfully on bacon strips from the prep table washed down with copious quaffs of root beer from the spigot behind the bar, tipping my glass so that the soda ran down the outside, resulting in a syrupy concentrate that lent me the wild vigour of an autistic child. I chuckled to think on all the sugar highs in that summer of wonders, and how in root beer sugar the cooking shifts were done and done again, as my life was done, because my *kennapy* was too small.

I sat on a cement abutment chattering like a rhesus to another skydiver who clearly owned his jump suit, and was trying to meditate, until a Cessna rattled up with a sticker on the dash that said NO FAT CHICKS. Inside, Bruce rode shotgun wearing a rubber hat shaped like a half-inflated football. The tail section was stripped of paneling; therein I hunkered with three other lads, all first-timers, all trying to look like Captain Kirk. The *ployne* hurtled heavenward, and we laughed! — at little things, such as the time, the view, and the old "unhook your ripcord while you're not looking" joke. Then Bruce threw wide the door and bellowed, buffeted by the dragony gale, "Are you *reddy?*"

But I was thinking of a plan to move out to the hinterland and grow a little garden like Lao Tzu if only God would let me live. I clamberered under the wing; my fingers claw the slippery strut. I can see all of Canada below, the True North, Strong and Free — so free they let the weak of mind jump out of a *ployne* after an hour of ritual gesturing.

CHAPTER XIV.

FREEDOM

A terrible accident — My last thoughts
of Guinevere — A true ghost story —
Farewell my love

BRUCE SHRIEKS *"GO!"* I DO NOT arch or count,
but only scream, my mind white as the Ice Age
at noon; I feel the elastic in my guts stretch both ways
and snap, then — *woosh!*

                        Like a tourist in my own
head I stare blankly up at something big: my *kennapy*,
fluttering like a paramilitary mandala, with sunlight
streaming through triangular holes. *I'm going to live!*

I gazed down over field and stream and saw the
beautiful woman swivel a big white arrow to show me
whither I should steer. Suddenly compelled to impress
her, I tugged on the steering toggles like Quasimodo,
down, down, like a bell ringing in the empty-headed
sky, until I dangled right above the X and the beautiful
woman was so impressed she jumped up and down and
shouted, "Let go of the toggles! Let go of the toggles!"

Too late! I hit the ground like a grand pee-*yannah*! My left knee crumpled like a Lucky™ beer can. I writhe on the dirt like a worm with boots on. My *ken-napy* fills with wind and slithers across the grass like a great beige jellyfish, trailing me after it, yelping like a dog with its leash caught in a car door, right past the beautiful woman, who's focused on the next jumper and does not even see me; then Guinevere comes running through the gentle grass, her face flushed with relief and pride.

Next day I feigned hale health and hobbled down Granville Street with her to the movies. We saw five in all, and between each we drank martinis, a thing we'd never done, so it was fun when it should have been sad; for this might be our last adventure.

The slanting light and smoky air recalled our first, five Octobers prior, when she was still married to my roomate Dave. Together with my gloomy Irish school-chum Bill we three had leased a clapboard antique on Redfern Street along the Oak Bay border, amidst a jigsaw puzzle of tree limbs and Tudor fascia whose gabled treetops held whole colonies of artists, angry feminists and members of failed cults.

Dave taught computer science at the University; so by 1982 our house was hooked up to the Internet — then a loose guild of university mainframes scattered across the globe — by a modem that sounded like a robot eating a piano. I drew tiny musical notes all day; Bill smoked, studied Hegel and *Playboy* and stared from his bedroom window at the FOR SALE sign on our lawn.

One morning I helped the old crone who lived two doors down wrestle a steamer trunk to her door. When

I turned to go she seized my arm and said with trembling lips her own sons were no help; in fact, they'd sued each other pre-emptively for the house, not even waiting till her death. I tried to escape, but she warned that my house, too, held tragic tales. Decades before a brother and sister had lived there. The girl was jilted at the altar and never left her room again. One week the brother did not come to work. The police found his corpse in Dave's room; his sister lay abed beside him, desiccated — for she'd been dead six months.

Guinevere nodded when she heard this. She'd sensed something was amiss; and I had too, for she paid no rent, and rarely washed the dishes, preferring to loll in leg warmers and a bra on Dave's big water bed, chortling, smoking, and reading *The Second Sex.* "It's clarified many of my own ideas," she said.

Just what we need, I thought, for she'd already used what theory she had to skirt both rent and housework. At least she might assist with heating. The walls were lath and plaster, the nights chill. On Hallowe'en Dave and I stole firewood from a neighbour's stack and huddled 'round the hearth. It was a blunt grey afternoon, and we could not convince the flames to catch. Then came a thump upstairs. No one heard save Guinevere and myself. We searched the house with no success, until the master bedroom.

By now a certain tension had built up on our adventure. The last place we looked was Dave's walk-in closet. Guinevere asked me to open the door, which I did with some unease. It was quite empty (Guinevere hung her clothes on chairs) but at the very back against the chimney wall we found an antique wedding dress.

I phoned the owner, who had been married in the

garden the summer before. She was mortified. How could she forget her own wedding dress? And why was it suddenly raining brides? Dead brides, forgetful brides — even Guinevere was suddenly a bride, standing beside me the altar in St. Andrew's Kirk downtown the following year. And now I waved her off to the Orient, then sat on the airport tiles and wept.

CHAPTER XV.

MODESTY

*Martin — Amsterdam — I encounter The
Voice — Funbags — A strange companion*

ENPLANED, I WOKE IN MY MODESTLY priced seat
somewhere over Iceland. Below the fuselage, in
the Atlantic darkness, Reagan and Gorbachev sat in
detente, each bent on forestalling Armageddon, each
with thirty thousand missiles aimed at the other. My
knee had puffed up like a python swallowing a child.
The tendons made strange clicks as I struggled to
adjust my sweat-dank cushion.

Wedged into steerage next to me dozed Martin,
a huge shambolic Dutchman with a wet red mouth
and scrubby neck-beard. We drank and snored and
watched the eastern glow split into red and yellow, an
angel Rothko; then alit in Europe *cantilevered* by a string
of tiny vodka bottles. Martin's brother found us at the
terminal and drove us in his dented compact through
forests marshalled straight as troops, to a gingerbread
train station in the heart of Amsterdam.

That town is where my memories begin. When I
was three my parents traded houses with a Dutch phy-
sician, and for a month I marvelled at the golden *guilder* coins, the chocolate milk, and the unfathomable

mystery of double-yolked eggs: how could the grocer know what lay within the shell?

Not just my personal consciousness but social conscience itself began in Amsterdam, which early legislated freedom of religion, the marketplace and the bedroom. Now those same freedoms had metastasized into a vast red-light district 'round the station. Coffee shops sold cake laced with hashish, and bored whores sat knitting in window displays nestled between pornographic book shops that catered to every deviance, including mine. It was a gimbler's Mecca — yet those delights were so admixed with every other perversion, of which I am repulsed as any, that the end result was not liberty, but nausea. Hell, as they say, is other peepholes.

I peg-legged back on wounded knee to the station, unable to outpace a ring of hopheads begging alms. One followed me into the *bureau de change*, his hair a-reek with sickly sweat, his nose whittled from a cuttlebone, his eyes sharp as talons on the teller tallying my *guilder*. "Oh-h!" he groaned and gnashed, "with just one of those I could buy a fix, I need my heroin, man! I'M SICK!"

The channel, flat and foggy, recalled a headline from the *London Times*:

FOG SHROUDS CHANNEL
CONTINENT ISOLATED

This captures the tone of Britain's *vox publica:* sly wit and open sarcasm, directed down at the masses, who perpetually work against their own best interests, and so must be protected from themselves, just as the world's first police force, London's bobbies, were conscripted to protect the indigent from each other, and also rich men's things.

By contrast the Voice of Canada is rational and detached as HAL 9000 (a part played by Canadian actor Douglas Rains), and so subtle it's often drowned out by the dogged bark of our neighbour to the south:

EXPLORE THE TWISTED WORLD OF
THE NAZIS FOR TEN DAYS — FREE!

My bus skirted the Thames along a concrete wall barbed with broken glass. Above the iron gate was writ HOME OF THE SUN. Below, twenty bobbies fiddled with plastic riot shields. This was the lair of Rupert Murdoch, who'd challenged the *vox publica's* singular and patrician tone with a *vox populi* of his own device (**THATCHER TO ARGENTINA: 'STICK IT UP YOUR JUNTA!'**) and in so doing, broke the trade union's grip on journalism, and later journalism itself. The bobbies stood guard lest disgruntled proles hurl Molotov cocktails at the *Sun* — yet everyone bought the rag because it said on the front:

BRITAIN'S FINEST FUN-BAGS!
(SEE PAGE THREE)

Those presently belonged to Samantha Fox, a blonde cockney whose peeler ilk I recalled with guilty pleasure from puberty, when they provided raw material for many an early gimbling scenario.

My bus entered a thicket of billboards depicting pickpockets (HE MIGHT BE RIGHT BEHIND YOU), car crash victims (SEATBELTS: COULDA, WOULDA, SHOULDA!) and badly-burnt children (YOU *HAD* THE CUTEST LITTLE BABY FACE), this last because Guy

Fawkes Night was almost upon us. We trundled into Victoria Station under a giant billboard of Samantha Fox in a tight tweed waistcoat, reading *The Times*:

TIME FOR A PAPER WITH
BETTER COVERAGE

I was hornswoggled. I'd grown up believing the *Sun* and *Times* were opposites, not supposed to touch. Now Murdoch owned them both; boobies and bobbies were complicit, and London was roiled by chaos: Reagan and Gorbachev had argued over Star Wars, their summit failed, and Pam found Bobby in the shower. She'd dreamt an entire season of *Dallas,* and Britons felt robbed by the Yanks — again! They still had not forgiven America for the War Debt, when Churchill borrowed billions from Roosevelt to rebuild, then watched as compound interest devoured the country's future. A constant refrain of the *vox publica* in my childhood had been that no matter how hard my generation worked, we'd never pay it off.

When I found the bus to Glasgow it was packed like a frat house phone booth, save for the adjacent seat. What luck! I might stretch out and sleep. But now an official-looking fellow checked a clipboard and stood aside to reveal a portly chap wearing a tweed capelet, deerstalker hat and bifocals thick as the bullseye glass in a *olde-worlde* pub window, who *harrumph'd* through his walrusy moustache and plopped down.

CHAPTER XVI.

ENTHUSIASM

*The Man-Child — Karl Marx — Great
Grannie gets knocked up — The return of
the native*

G ALUMPHING WITH ENTHUSIASM 'round the tiny
seating space, my new friend espied a small closed-
circuit television dangling from the luggage rack and
cried, "TB! TB!" then seized my copy of *Nicholas Nick-
elby* and chortled, "*TB Guide? TB Guide?* Hmm? Hah!
BLEURRRGH!"

I wrested Dickens from his tree-root fingers and
turned in desperation to the window. The bus had
stalled on a long, curved street lined with furniture
shops and newsstands. The way forward was blocked
by a shirtless white-haired man in worsted jacket
and paisley underpants, who grated his teeth at two
approaching orderlies. My companion guffawed and
pointed at the lunatic, squashing my face against the
pane until I felt I was become the filling in a madness
sandwich.

The blockader was carried off, the bus rolled
on, and my friend sat quietly until his restless hands
decanted the ashtray onto my thigh. He tried to rub
the ash away as forcefully as if he were inventing fire,
until I seized his wrists, upon which tears welled in his

eyes and splashed down into his moustache. I laughed despite myself, and he did too, then fell asleep.

I glanced up at the little television and asked the conductor if there would be a movie. "Not likely," he said. "The TV's broke and the tapes got stole."

Instead he sold me gammon sandwiches from a box, or tried, for my companion roused with a sudden roar and flung himself into the aisle, seized the box and shook it till the sandwiches fell out while my fellow passengers glared and wondered why I did not better control my charge.

Till Manchester the man-child was rendered docile by improvised finger-puppet entertainments while we rolled through histories personal and profound. A century ago this town and its environs were home to a third of the world's cotton mills, and clothed the human family. Karl Marx wrote his manifesto among that standing army of displaced proles, the working

poor, with whom he sympathized. For he too was poor; his wife was poor; his five children were poor; even his maid was poor — so indigent and chilly Marx took her to his bed and warmed her there, and sired a son on her, whom he later disowned for his low station. Some say, "What of it? Marx was a class warrior, not a class act." But that maid might have been my own great-grandmother, who was born into a Newcastle slum so desperate the upstairs neighbour once suckled a rat, believing it to be her infant (it's said the rodents smell the milk and burrow under the sheets to feed).

Great-grannie's life was hard: her mother died; her stepfather paid the twopenny fee for his own daughters' schooling, but not for hers. At eleven she was indentured to a mansion, whose scion "knocked her up" when she was twelve.

The infant was removed to an orphanage and by chance the fallen woman-child met my great-grand-father, who'd come to study the steam-powered paper mills in Manchester. The two fled north to Gretna Green on the Scottish border, which was the Vegas of its day. A man might marry there at fourteen without parental consent, and not postpone his passion until England's ripe old majority of seventeen.

The border regions, which the bus now breached at high speed, were forested once with oaks so dense that even Rome threw up Her hands, then Hadrian's Wall. The Picts beyond were deemed the fiercest savages in the ancient world (except the Welsh, against whose sharpened sticks the Romans also built a barricade — the lesser-known Antonine's Wall, just four feet high, yet still a Welshman could not clear it. Morwen and David grew up at one end of it. "A gloomy spot," said

Morwen. "Dark.")

This landscape of love and horror was now redacted into strips of sodden grass and gray concrete punctured by lonely petrol kiosks. The roadway rolled beneath the bus like a tarmacadam hamster wheel till Glasgow lummoxed from the north. I stepped down into the city of my birth; a ring of Scots looked up at me and cheered, then shouldered me aside and ringed the man-child, embracing him as he wept with joy.

The bus station sat on a rubbled hill under a chocolate sodium sky. On the far slope stood what might be the University, where my Uncle Stanley taught teaching. But all seemed out of joint. Whither the sooty walls and gargoyles of that industrial cathedral, Glasgow Central? The porter jerked his thumb at the building we stood beside, now scoured the colour of shortbread, as if burnt toast had been scraped into a sink. Within, time stood partly still: something electronic had replaced the great timetable where I'd once watched men undertake by hand

> *The application of these train departure times:*
> *Letters on a big, black board.*

Yet the stone walls were still set with windows cribbed from some ruined cathedral, and at the platform's end there still came that dreamlike moment when trains roared from within a church to without a railway station. On one of these I rode through various sooty cuttings and tunnels to Queen's Park and limped the last three blocks to 40 Westmoreland Street, my ancestral tenement home.

CHAPTER XVII.

FOLLOWING

*The tenement — Uncanny Grannie —
Hugh and Sheila — Blind!*

I WOKE THE FOLLOWING afternoon and stared up at the Italian plasterwork on the ceiling of my Grannie's so-called "Big Room". In a childhood shuffled and dealt between three continents, this tenement had been the only constant — my almost-home; yet there was something uncanny about the place, and also about Grannie. Unlike my modest mother she wore *décolletage*, which to my untrained six-year-old eye made of her chest a "plumber's crack", so that I imagined she might either sit or lie face-down upon a toilet seat.

She had a gammy leg from tumbling down the corkscrew stairs on a double-decker bus. The woman behind her tripped too, and stabbed her stiletto heel into the flesh between Grannie's calf and bone. Thanks to the National Health medical care was free; but her sister Mary had gone once to the Western Infirmary and never come back. So Grannie took no chances, and bound her leg with lint and sticking plaster. The wound had festered fifty years.

To douse the pain she crushed codeine into a spoon

each morning, and took a double dose before retiring to her bed in a curtained niche off the kitchen — alone, for Grandfather had died of lung cancer years before.

In the strange sad shire of my prepubescence, when I'd begun to grasp the nature of my gimbling habit and could not sleep for fear, she drugged me with codeine and we drowsed together in that recess; wrapped in the liniment arms of night I tumbled through interlocking hells of comic book intestines and snarling clocks.

Now my uncanny Grannie had shrunk to the size

CODEINE NIGHTMARE № 616

of a bird, and the tenement had shrunk with her. The "Big Room" was so attenuated I could not turn around with my rucksack on, yet the chambers seemed tall as before. Built so the foul air from gas lamps and coal fires would not kill the tenants, the ceiling stretched so far away it seemed like another country.

Aged nine I found if I hung like a bat from the back

of a chair for twenty minutes my brain adapted and the room swung topsy-turvy, so that up was down, then watched in wonder as adults strode around the ceiling the Italian plasterwork on the floor grew up around the stalagmite lamps.

I breakfasted on butter and bacon then hied with Grannie to visit Uncle Charlie, a rubicund and cheerful fellow who'd spent the war cutting burnt bodies out of crashed planes at Hertfordshire Airfield yet came through his ordeal unscathed, the family thought, till one night he was found in a ditch beside the Great Western Road, blind drunk and hauling ghost bodies from imaginary planes.

The great joy of his life was Hugh, his son, born handsome, glad and big. When I turned ten Hugh married Sheila, whose golden skin and sooty lashes betrayed Italian lineage. They wed at a hotel in King's Park, where melon balls were served in cocktail glasses, and the couple kissed in front of everyone. "This is what love looks like," I thought.

They bought a flat in the West End, where even their furniture held the promise of the Future: for it was imbued with modern design, with no overhangs where the crab-thing might hide. At last I could stand up and mosey from the couch like any normal child, a ray of light in a dark world, for I'd begun to fear I would go blind. There was no evidence for this; but who could say what might befall me in the future? Perhaps, the worst! My brother, already the doctor in the family, examined my pupils and shook his head. "They're unnaturally enlarged," he said.

So there was no hope. Soon I'd be blind as the insides of a radio play. Blind as the soles of Samuel Beckett's shoes. Blind as Aunt Kate, whose eyes were scabbed with cataracts — although in compensation she'd been gifted with second sight. At tea time she would read the leaves left in the dregs for any neighbour who had questions on their destiny, excepting children, whose tomorrows were so thronged with possibility that their tea leaves swirled like snow.

At twenty-two Hugh's cup still held naught but snow, perhaps because so many options lay ahead. Already

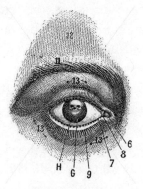

he was accredited as an accountant, and soon there would be children.

At twenty-three he died of leukæmia. The Minister who married them buried him and tried to comfort her, following her to the school where she taught and lurking behind railings until, unable to shake him off, she married him. The family lost touch, but the pinstriped suit that Hugh had cut for his accounting work passed down to me.

CHAPTER XVIII

REPAIRING

*The Scientific Method — Hobbes: Nasty,
British and short — Swift — Scots invent
the Future — Lilith*

N EXT DAY I REPAIRED TO the scullery, where on
the worn Formica™ countertop, at six, I acciden-
tally discovered the scientific method. My father was
still in Africa; my mother took my sister to the doctor,
and I was trusted for the first time to come home from
school alone and make my lunch.

On the cracked counter I found bread and one
boiled egg, set apart from five raw ones. I spun the
eggs, enjoying their wobbled motion — then realized
I had mixed mine in with all the others. I could not
find my lunch without cracking them all. Wasting
eggs was then a capital offence: Grannie would *skelp*
me, just as she'd *skelped* my mother constantly, with
the methodical brutality of a first-class mind forced to
travel steerage.

I spun eggs glumly and fell into my *wyrd* — that spell
that came upon me when I drew, or pored o'er pictures
of the stars. As my mind moved upon silence I saw
one egg spun differently from the rest: less wobbly it
was. Exactly one of the six? Surely that could not be
chance. I cracked the shell over the sink and found . . .

my lunch!

As I ran back to Annett Street School the spring air seemed to thrill with invisible Laws of Science. I'd seen inside an egg! as clearly as if I'd purchased X-ray glasses from the back page of a Batman comic; and this superpower had saved me from a *skelping*. Yet while Scotland's branches held the Future aloft, its roots reached down to savagery. As late as 1930, on

the Westernmost Isle of St. Kilda — a rocky chalice thrust up from the sea — the locals lived much as they had since Jesus wore his jagged hat, scrabbling bare-foot on the thousand-foot cliffs in search of puffin meat and potatoes. Yet James Watt invented steam power in his mother's scullery in much the same way I had found my lunch: lost in reverie, he watched a pot lid wobble up and down.

This last seems no great feat of deductive reason;

and in truth the Greeks invented steam power two millennia prior, but used it only to operate toys and temple doors. And who can fault them? Steam power would have bequeathed to Athens only an army of disenfranchised slaves. But in Britain, whose Commonwealth sought a new social contract with its citizens, the result was a great liberation, a transformation of Hobbes's Leviathan masses, seen on that 1651 tome's frontispiece as entirely subsumed inside the gigantic State, into Swift's Lilliputians of 1726: that band of tiny locals who seek to constrain the giant Gulliver when he awakens on their faraway beach.

It is as if these iconic images document the rise of the Individual, stirred from slumber, outnumbered but enormous, who easily overcomes the masses, now outside of him, multifold yet tiny.

From this fertile ground sprung Hume's Progressive

philosophy; Smith's unseen hand; Bell's telephone; Logie-Baird's television; and McAdam's macadam. Clearly, reason was in the very sod. Scotland's Celtic Otherness alone cannot explain this, for the Welsh are Celts, yet their idea of progress is replacing children with pit ponies. Some other unseen hand must account for it — perhaps the "clean slate" provided by Culloden, when Scottish swords went up against English guns, and within an hour the clans were slain, sorted by kilt and shovelled into mass graves. Freed from the ancient clan system, a thousand Futures bloomed.

But these had turned around and bitten the unseen hand. The country was now a testing ground for Progress. Lest it explode and hurt someone, the first experimental nuclear reactor was built Dounrey, a beach at the north tip of Scotland, where its white dome bulged from the sedge like a tumour on tomorrow's brow. Inside, a glass case perilously close to the tea shop's donuts held a Bronze Age skeleton exhumed by the builders. Where's the respect? The Concorde's secret test flights were routed over our little town of Golspie. We heard the boom and thought the Judgement was at hand. And now Whitehall had leased the Holy Loch to host America's nuclear submarine fleet, in partial payment of the War Debt ... but I forgot these woes when my boyhood crush, Lilith, called on the telephone.

CHAPTER XIX.

THE APPROACH

*Lilith vs. Guinevere — My mother arrives
— Funny about Hitler — The love of
ruins*

S O GORGEOUS I HAD NOT DARED APPROACH HER in
our tweens, Lilith had understudied on the London
stage for Sarah Brightman, to whom she bore uncanny
resemblance. We met for lunch; but the affair was
botched by Guinevere, who suddenly appeared in my
head, so that I thought on how she liked me to make
the bed on top of her by wafting the sheets down from
above; her perfect bite, which a dentist used to model
false teeth; and how she read *Shogun* in a day. Thus
nothing came of lunch with Lilith.

I set out to find the house where I was born. I
had a notion the sight would better anchor me in the
world, but reached the place to find it gone, become
a motor-highway. I sat in a *kebab* shop and gazed
through the metal grille at traffic. It looked like rain,
for which Scots have more words than Inuit have for
snow. Specifically, the day was *dreech:* overcast with a
chance of doom.

I walked on to the second place I'd lived: Cumber-
nauld, a "new town" built to replace the tenement
slums, planned, like the Soviet economy, by techno-

crats. The playgrounds were sandpits whose structures channeled every kind of Scottish rain into their
bowels, filled up with bacteria like vast petri dishes
and infected every child for miles. Chunks of culvert
remaindered from construction were arranged into
adventure playgrounds; said adventure comprised leaping from pipe to pipe like Mario Brothers in anoraks
until the child would smash his shins against the edge
of one, and roll in agony on the germy sand, cursing
God and the architects, who had won prizes worldwide but never had to live in the abomination they had
wrought.

I hobbled back to Westmoreland Street and found
my mother arrived from the North, where she'd been
visiting with friends. From her I had inherited my love
of story; listening to her put me in a sort of trance, as
she told of lying abed during the Blitz on nights when
Hitler's bombs lit the sky from dusk till dawn, praying
it might last past midnight so she'd have the day off
school; and of how my Uncle Bomey tumbled from a
tenement roof into a huge pile of soot, yet lived; and
of the woman upstairs who beat her little husband till
he bled then threw him out into the rain, and when
the *polis* knocked her door her big arm would emerge
holding his jacket and hat; and of the harelipped dock-
worker with pincers for hands and feet, a human Crab
Thing whose five daughters suffered the same genetic
fate, wore socks over their hands, and scuttled across
the floors of the windowless tenement rooms above.

When she told these tales it was as if they were hap-
pening to her now. Her great joy was writing essays;
but at fifteen her mother took her out of school and put
her to work in a window cleaner's office, despite the

Headmaster's objections. "She's the best student in the class," he said at Sports Day; but Grannie's mind was made up: boys go to school, women to work. My mother never complained, preferring to stay on good terms with everyone — only she was a little funny about Hitler.

Next evening she and I caught trains in opposite

directions. On the front stoop Grannie reached up and cupped my face, and we both saw it was the end: we'd never meet again.

The tenements we passed by taxi *en route* to Glasgow Central had been scrubbed of their black glistening soot as part of Thatcher's plan to revitalise the State. Gone were the miles of bombed-out ruin, where wallpaper and fireplaces could be seen three stories up, and when the vesp'ral sun shone through the sandstone formed a landscape haunting as the cover of *Dhalgren*.

My mother chatted with the cabbie, and before we reached the station he had told us his life story: taxed by all, tipped by none. "Imagine if you had to work for two dollars an hour," he said, and laughed aloud at my plan to find employment in the South.

"You won't find work in London, laddie! Grown men are living on the street for want of a job."

The red-eye shunted out of Glasgow Central past a wall of tenements pocked with bright-lit windows; then the scene was hidden by a tunnel wall, just as it had been twenty years before, the night we left for Africa, upon which Father said, "That's the last you'll see of Glasgow for years."

CHAPTER XX.

CONTEMPLATION

*Red-eye to London — Reminiscences of
the Pearl of Africa — The Great Dictator
and the Yellow Bird — Democracy —
Corruption*

A S I CONTEMPLATED THIS personal palimpsest
in the buffet car I fell into conversation with two
big Londoners, who set six tall Guinness cans on the
tiny table, wedged their massive frames into their doll-
house seats and began to chatter, then promptly fell
asleep. In the sudden quiet of the carriage I tried to
envision my future; but my mind snagged like a tongue
against a tooth on things long past. I felt I'd set some
great recapitulation in motion with that walking tour
of my childhood, and this might carry me to Africa,
for which place I'd yearned — not the hell-hole racked
by AIDS, but the Eden to which I'd jetted in the Sixties.

The airliner to Cairo had silver tea service and jig-
saws. I tore up the box lids, which spoiled that sacred
moment when my whole perspective shifted with a
sudden *click!* as disparate chunks fit into place, and
set to work. In Cairo a steward tried to take the jigsaw back, but I refused. It wasn't done. They all but
held the plane until I finished. Above the Sudan our
propellors thrilled to an electric storm that tossed the
plane around the sky like a shuttlecock. Then in Kam-

pala a *concierge* black as a boot, his jacket rowed with gold buttons, picked me up from where I lay fatigued upon the carpet of the Speke Hotel, named for the explorer John Speke, who with the great Sir Richard Burton — the explorer, not the actor — discovered the Nile's source.

Burton was fearless, save when it came to honey. After they dined with friends he told his wife, "I could not relax. I sensed there was honey in the room, and feared they might think me mad if I asked for its remove."

I knew exactly how he felt. At six, I had to know which clothes I would be wearing in the week ahead or I could not relax. My mother must lay them out in patterns on my bed; only after inspecting them did I feel at ease. She, conversely, was at her wit's end. Of nervous disposition, she now must raise two little boys in a jungle that was always trying to eat us, along with a babe-in-arms, my little sister, whose first teeth were removed *sans* analgesic, so rustic were conditions in our region.

To combat the endemic poverty a local leader arose: Milton Obote, born into a tribal situation in the Apac district to the north, and educated in Marx and Rousseau. He believed in the power of the ballot box to such an extent that every polling station had two: the first held votes for him, the second, a list of miscreants who must be beaten with a hammer after the election; which task was undertaken by Obote's Number Two, a hulking country lad named Idi Amin Dada.

Amin had been trained by the British Army, and his hammer skills were not uncommon, for instead of the Rule of Law Uganda practised rough justice. Once in

the market I saw a shoplifter caught by a mob. They threw bricks at him, then a bicycle. Policemen chased the mob away, picked up that bricked, biked thief, beat him more bloody still, and hurled him into their van.

A week later when my father was pickpocketed in the market he had to stop himself from shouting, "Stop, thief!" as he might in Britain, for fear another mob might beat the miscreant to death. Despite such chicanery he loved his new position, at a school that prepped country boys for entrance to the British university system. He was also the games officer, so when one of his students, a go-getter named Jolly Roger, proposed they throw a dance, my father went down to the local jazz club in Jinja — which, like all such in Uganda, employed without irony the title *Gay Life Saloon* — and hired the only jazz quartet for miles. Anon, Amin arrived to hire the band for the same night. The bartender feared a hammering, so agreed

— and, as was the custom of that place, simply hoped the situation would resolve itself.

The big night came, the base boomed "Yellow Bird" at the competing crickets, the equatorial stars shone tangled in elephant grass, and a platoon of soldiers marched onto the dance floor. Amin had sent them to collect the band. A not-so-jolly Roger borrowed ten shillings from my father and bribed the sergeant; the platoon repaired to the *Gay Life Saloon* and drank the night to sleep.

From this my father gleaned *graft* meant something different here. Consider the Chief Executive at Jinja Nile Textiles Cooperative, who came to work one day in a Mercedes — a "minister's car", the sort of Black Maria that government actors drove in cavalcades up and down our only paved stretch of road, between Kampala and Entebbe, with tiny flags a-flying. This was their idea of civil service. The Benz insignia was so identified with power that one afternoon our own Mercedes was caught up in Obote's fleet, hemmed in by outriders through the Jinja roundabout, unable to escape. But the Head of the Co-operative was no minister. Where did he get the CASH? He'd siphoned the entire operating budget of the company into his family's coffers.

A week after he was caught he stood at the bus stop with the workers he had cheated. None blamed him: they would all have done the same. A man who does not use his power to benefit his kin is not a man at all. This is not corruption: they simply dance to a different drummer. And reminiscing fondly on that beat, I suddenly hoped my future lay in dancing to it also.

CHAPTER XXI

DECIDING

Denmark Hill — Nigel, the over-educated
handyman — Stephen & Sung-ha

THAT NIGHT I DECIDED to set a course for Africa. But first I needed CASH!, for my cook's wages were near spent. I arrived in London with only one resource: a scrap of paper scribbbled with the address of my best friend, Stephen, presently in London, and living on Denmark Hill.

The road up to his flat was prosperous and leafy on the right, where stood a row of old brick houses studded with round red fire alarms, as though each wore a medal. On close inspection these were burglar alarms; for across the street squatted a platoon of dismal council flats walled in by razor wire.

Stephen was not home, but Nigel, the superintendant, let me in. The room's French doors opened on gardens trimmed neat as Versailles, with cinder paths and boxwood hedges that smelled of cat. Nigel said the French doors were a security nightmare, thanks to all the burglars who lurked across the street. I said Stephen was an art student; there was naught to burglarize. Nigel said I did not grasp the current state of affairs; I said I did: it was a state of mind. Consider the pickpocket billboard I'd seen on the bus (HE MIGHT BE RIGHT BEHIND YOU). The thief's giant face — a collage of ears and eyes — suggested he might be anyone; yet all his parts were black or tan, suggesting otherwise. In Canada the image would be deemed racist. Nigel countered that there were so few Englishmen left in London it would be more racist if any of the parts were white.

He plied me with warm beer, and I was amazed to learn the kitchen furniture I'd deemed so shoddy was in fact priceless and antique. Even the plain little spice rack I broke once I was drunk turned out to be an ashwood heirloom from the estate of D.H. Lawrence, which lay just up the road from Nigel's country place.

He spoke eloquently for a handyman, and in the accent of the British upper-working class (sometimes erroneously called the middle class), his glottals polished smooth by international affairs into a *Transatlantic*. He fiddled with a three-pronged plug so big it might have been struck from the set of *Aida*, yet had only a rudimentary idea of how electricity worked. What kind of superintendant was he?

Nigel shook his sheepy curls and said in a single breath by trade he was a nuclear engineer who'd run a reactor that ten years back malfunctioned and flushed a million gallons of coolant into a nearby slough; the following day reporters from the *Sun* parked vans around his office and ran at him across macadam with their ties a-flap while the telephone rang and a deep Thatcherian Voice at the other end told him to say nothing, which he did, until his nerves collapsed like a circus tent and he was forced to plough his severance into this leaky garden flat, whose rooms he let to students, for he'd loved his university days, but there was no money in it, and he might be burglarized at any moment, and what did I think of London?

I told him I could wait outside if he had things to do. But he would not hear of it. Well after dark, Stephen arrived with his new Korean bride Sung-ha. We'd met as lads, in 1974, at the Canada-Russia hockey games — a gambit designed to ease the tension between East and West through sport. At our school gym the student body splayed in daisy chains 'round televisions set on the polished floor. Stephen said hello, and that the scar on his throat was from an emergency tracheotomy, as he'd been born with a scorching fever and laid upon a bed of ice while a priest was summoned, for unbaptized Catholic babes are banished into limbo, where they float forever in the wailing dark. His parents had higher hopes for him, so let the priest perform both first and last rites. But he cheated God and survived, and now studied opera in London with Sung-ha.

He was delighted by my top-hat rabbit appearance; Sung-ha, less so. He was dismayed to hear Guinevere was not with me; Sung-ha, more so. But both laughed merrily when I ate a box of ice cream bars and barfed them up again onto the railway track. At the local pub Stephen read me a review in *Time Out: London*, of Sung-ha's latest near-triumph as a *chanteuse*: "A more easily-dazzled jury might have chosen the charismatic Korean," said the text, and called her doll-like — which she was: a tiny gold-skinned voodoo creature, pulling strings behind the scenes: for no matter what decisions were made, or how strategies played out upon the ground, her objective was always met.

But she was fun, and next day we three wended by double decker to the National Gallery to visit the famous Cartoon by Leonardo DaVinci — a man I much admired, though for unusual reasons.

DA VINCI'S CARTOON

CHAPTER XXII

GRACE

*Leonardo — The Duchenne smile —
Minimum wage in London — A battle
with the Forces of Chaos*

HE LIVED IN A STATE OF GRACE in an Age of Wholeness, when Art and Science were one. No wallflower, Da Vinci considered his greatest triumph not Mona Lisa but the weaponization of mediæval Italy: first on his *curriculum vitæ* came "manufacturer of arms". Even Mona Lisa is part science, for he used the selfsame trick June showed me on the roof of Elliot Building, that I might better glimpse Saturn by averting my eye, to create history's most mysterious smile.

Recall the *foveæ's* cones are built to catch detail but need much light, while the surrounding rods need little light but provide scant detail. Da Vinci used this to make Mona Lisa's smile vanish and reappear, to wit: a smile's as complex as an eye: false smiles lie only in the mouth — the salesman's rictal grin. A smile that fills both mouth and eye is called a *Duchenne smile*: here, the observer's gaze flits up and down between eyes and mouth to test if the smiler is sincere.

When Mona Lisa's eyes are viewed from just the right remove, light from the corners of her mouth falls not on the observer's *foveæ*, but on the surrounding rods.

Detail is lost; the shadows below her cheeks merge to give the impression of a smile. When the observer's eyes flick to her mouth to check this smile, *presto!* It's gone. This mimics the *subtle interplay* of eye and mouth in a Duchenne smile.

To create his masterpiece Da Vinci must needs grasp both the physical structure of the eye and the emotional structure of the smile. He was not artist nor scientist, but master of both; and not in the manner of a man who masters chewing gum and strolling. As with the Duchnne smile, it is the *subtle interplay* of art and science that makes the mystery whole, and earns him that sobriquet of genius polymaths: Renaissance Man. A humbler version of the same was my dream; but it was an untimely one, for I lived in an Age of Experts. Also, I must find a job.

London is massive and sprawling and never sleeps, like a big-boned woman on Benzedrine™. For years she'd languished at the fag-end of Keynesian *largesse*. But that year, 1986, came the Big Bang, wherein Thatcher and her neo-conservative cabal deregulated the banks, and now the City was changing faster than the water in a broken toilet.

I found a post at once in Britain's fastest-growing industry. They needed night guards; and like many an Outsider, I nursed a secret fancy where I was furnished with a hat and gun, and charged not with thought crimes but with laying down the State's hegemony. I saw the job as a battle with the Forces of Chaos. Also, I might sometimes nap unheeded.

Cyclops Security (not their real name) comprised a tiny room in Ravenscourt full of men with phones crooked in their necks, all sticking pins into a giant wall map of London, as if battling the Blitz with voodoo. The company chief was Barney, a woman so massively built she's lost her foothold in my memories, and through them drifts in her white blouse, an angry iceberg.

Barney welcomed me aboard and sent me to the outfitters, who swathed me in navy nylon: parka, hat, trousers, and sweater with epaulettes, all crackling from the cleaners. Then I was shot through the Tube to a half-built television station near Elephant & Castle, where the day guard briefed me: "There's the couch. There's an alarm clock hid under the cushion. Just make sure you're awake when the Branch Manager comes 'round in the *mornink*."

I soon learned there was no battle with the Forces of Chaos: the battle was to sleep as long as you could before the Branch Manager caught you. The men of Cyclops had developed sleeping on the job into a science. Some rolled up carpets into makeshift beds; others pulled chairs together to make a sort of hammock. The man at the Waverly Biscuit Factory had an army cot hanging down an air shaft on a rope. The *rasta* who ran Visa™ HQ slept right on the big computer desk under a pointillist *mappa mundi* made from a thousand tiny lightbulbs. He said, "Don't worry about the Branch Manager, mon. With these closed-circuit TV cameras we can see 'im coming for miles."

He dropped his scratchy nylon pants and let his white shirt billow like a jib sail in the dark. I slept on the floor until the wee hours, then woke to find him
plucking the hairs on my arm, his toothy grin
a floating band of white that, at my
frightened glance, retreated
like the Cheshire Cat,
into th'electric
darkness.

CHAPTER XXIII

STRIPPING

*I begin to lose my mind — Tony — Sam
Fox — The AIDS conspiracy — A
runaway — The Great Wall of Fraser —
I get into a fight*

EACH NIGHT I STRIPPED DOWN to my shirt and slept; each day I drew at divers museums. Each shift saw me in a different region of the city. One night I was at Wembley, fast asleep; the next at the Hotel Savoy downtown, where another man from Cyclops, Tony, sat in a small guard room near the cellar door, his tie knotted like parcel string, his face flushed and creased, as if he'd recently stretched out and slept right on the desk beneath a massive poster of Samantha Fox. Each of her breasts was bigger than my head. That was not big enough for Tony. He climbed up on a stool and gawked, then saw her skin was downed with tiny hairs. "I don't like that," he said. "You want a woman to be *smoove*."

I said such foliation was *de rigeur* for primates like ourselves, to which he added that monkeys were responsible for AIDS. "The CIA was testing stuff on a monkey down in Africa — left the bloody cage door open! Bloody monkey escapes and bites a bloody Arab. Bloody Arab comes to London, gives it to about a *fousand* bloody prostitutes, and now a million Brits is dead! They should shut down the bloody channel is *wot!*"

I passed the following night in a ruined priory outside Finchley. A crucifix hung above the entrance near a developer's sign that said COMING SOON. Within there mouldered stories of ruptured floorboards and sagging wallpaper. The Branch Manager said thieves had tried to use the place as a hideout. I roamed the hallways with my torch until I found a sodden mattress and pile of clothes — the villains' lair! On the mattress lay a note:

> *I know you are afrade of him*
> *but you* MUST *come home,*
> > *love Mum.*

At dawn I wrote: PROTECTED RICH MAN'S STUFF FROM FRIGHTENED CHILD in the log book. At dusk I was hauled before Barney, who shook her jowls and said, "That log book is a legal document. We might have to read it out in court!" She lacked the manpower to fire me, but as punishment I was sent to the House of Fraser, where there had been "a bit of trouble".

I spent the day at the National Gallery, drowsing on the bench in front of *Sunday in the Park* until the docent shook my foot and whispered, "You can't sleep here."

No loss — I'd sleep at work. That night I squeezed through the Tube onto a street hedged with trees through whose bald crowns roared wet gusts filled with the hiss of traffic tires. The House of Fraser was cold as an undersea cave. The vaulted ceiling was gilt plaster; the main floor was divided by a plywood wall. Through a square peephole I glimpsed the men of a rival company with nicer hats and greatcoats who guarded the other half of the building. A fellow Cyclops sat on a metal chair and fumed in blank Cockney: "Ponses! Who needs a coat like that to guard a bloody building, ey?" He opened a paperback entitled *MURDER*.

"What's it about?" I asked.

"I don't care," he said, "so long as there's blood. I looooove blood." Beside him a ball-faced man named Simon tipped his chair back. His accent was lower-middle-working class; he was the sort who might have sold a used Mini Countryman™ to any of my uncles. He'd written for the *News of the World* till he was sent to interview a London cabbie whose daughter had been raped, and found himself defenestrated.

"It was the ground floor," he said, smoking. Still, it had left a mark. But now he'd befriended an older man whose business laminated paper products, and who had stomach cancer and no children. Simon stood to inherit the lot! This happy chat was interrupted by the Branch Manager. He'd driven all the way from Canterbury to explain last night's "trouble."

"Thieves came over the wall right there at two in the morning," he puffed rapidly as he showed me round the doors and other weak points in our defences. "They overpowered our lads and stole a box of Mars™ bars from the caf."

Had he informed the police? No, no, this was an internal affair. And tonight we must be vigilant, in case those thieves returned. He, on the other hand, must return to Canterbury at once — a drive that would take hours, and cost him money, and he had a sore back, and the rain was dreadful. Dreadful!

I took the three-bar electric fire into a changing room and curled up on the freezing carpet, but did not sleep a wink before the Branch Manager from the rival company came bashing through a hole in the plywood wall, declaiming loudly of slander and incompetence. How dare we accuse his men of theft? Five men now shouted at each other across the plywood wall, as if this were a toy Berlin. Exhausted, I said aloud what we all knew: guards from the other company had stolen the Mars™ bars while our lads slept. And which offence might more concern the police?

At the dread word, the other aged ten years. He shrank a foot, his lank hair thinned, his skin went gray. "No need for that," he mumbled, and stood down, revealing Simon, who silently guffawed in the middle distance.

Next day I nodded on a couch in the Tate Modern until I rolled onto the hardwood floor with a coconut *clunk!* At dusk I hastened to HQ, and yet again was hauled in front of Barney. Simon had informed her of last night's standoff. I steeled for discharge, but:

"That's the stuff," she said, and sent me to a plum position, whence I hurtled through miles of crumbling tunnels, like a salmon spawning in a bricked-up river, until I surfaced near Blackfriar's Bridge clutching the crumpled company map, on which a black "X" marked the spot.

CHAPTER XXIV

THE TURNING POINT

An evening at Sainsbury's — Australian dreams — A Union "fing" — I help abuse some blacks

XALSO MARKED THE TURNING point of my career in law enforcement: a place called Sainsbury's™, which I had never heard of, and imagined might be a strip club, or better yet, a featherbed factory. But Barney's notion of a plum was the opposite of mine. Sainsbury's™ comprised a desk beside a window that looked out on more brick, in a lobby where there would be no chance to sleep.

The day guard's accent was upper-middle-working class; he might have been a council member or a teacher, had those positions not been retired.

"You're from Canada!" he said. He too had dreams of emigration — not to Canada, God no! he hated snow — but to Australia! He loved the place! He drank Australian wine! He watched Australian films! and look! He pulled an Australian magazine from a valise. The cover showed a sunny shore. I asked when he would ship out. He shook his head.

"It's just a dream! Unless I marry a rich Australian woman!" He chuckled in a way that spoke of many happy hours spent scanning antipodean personal ads, then left without appraising me of what Sainsbury's™ was, or did.

At midnight a bevy of businessmen shuffled down the stairs, followed by labourers in boiler suits, then laughing women in lab coats. The lobby's backlit floor plan was no help: MAINFRAME COMPUTERS — LABS 33-66 — DANGER! RADIATION! What was Sainsbury up to?

THE BIG SMOKE

The glass door wobbled; a little Cockney with a shock of sandy hair, white sideburns, and a nose as pink and fleshy as a newborn mouse wheeled in a massive metal box.

"Ninety-nine tins of jam," he said. We checked our manifold lists, compared serial numbers, filled out forms with blunt and stubby pencils, put everything into an envelope, twisted its metal seal shut and stuffed it through a hole in the front of the box dark as a Crusader's eye slot. It seemed a lot of paperwork for jam. The cockney wheeled the tin box down the hall, parked it outside a double door, and left. An hour later he returned with ninety-nine *bananars*. Why ninety-nine? I asked. He said because that number was divisible by three — they needed two *bananars* for each test and one for the *control*.

Behind my desk was an alcove. I rolled my chair back into it, shoved down my hat and tried to sleep. Moments later the back wall of the alcove shot aside and a man in a tall white chef's hat appeared. He asked if I would like a Salisbury steak for seventeen pence. I said the price seemed low. He nodded. "It's been divided by ten. It's a Union *fing*."

I ate the steak; the Cockney returned with ninety-nine sweaters; I wheeled them down the hall to find the *bananars* gone. Already I saw Barney's jowls shake: "All you had to do was guard those ninety nine *bananars!*"

The glass door wobbled, and the cleaning crew came in — all black women with smiles as white as shells on a lava beach. They mopped and sprayed and chatted in *patois* about the bus to Brixton, then the security division of the cleaning company arrived — all white men in off-the-rack suits, who began to strip search the black women, because last week one had been caught with two rolls of toilet paper under her coat.

I wanted to take a moral stand, but on what grounds? I had no idea what Sainsbury's™ was, or did, save test *bananars*. And, DANGER! RADIATION? Perhaps it was a matter of national security. Also, I was a gimbler, and exhausted. So I sat behind my desk like a wallflower at a Nazi bundt until the last black woman had been rifled and flushed into the street; then the alcove wall shot sideways and the cook appeared, wagging his tall white hat. Did I want breakfast for ten pence? I did.

He led me down a stairwell through tunnels walled with massive pipes and up into a cafeteria wide as a school gymnasium, where crowds rushed upon countertops laden with Sainsbury's™ sausage, Sainsbury's™ eggs and Sainsbury's™ corn flakes, and all the prices had been divided by ten, except the Chia Pets™, which were free.

I knew that night I must soon leave the land of my birth, or die in the attempt. At the local pub the crowd sat dumb as mummers staring at the TV, whereon Noel Edmonds, whose popular programme badgered chubby Britons into performing foolhardy stunts, was now emroiled in scandal: a hefty bricklayer had died that night while bungee-jumping from an exploding box suspended fifty yards above a street in Cheapside. The *Sun* had Edmonds declaim: **IT'S ALL MY FAULT!** I did not know Edmonds from Adam, yet I had seen this show before, in 1973, when World Cup goalie Gordon Banks crashed his sports car and told the *Times*: IT'S ALL MY FAULT!

It must be something in the air, or soil; whate'er the cause, its effect on me was toxic as lead.

CHAPTER XXV.

UNEMBROILING

The happy couple — I talk with Guinevere
— A big decision — Heathrow

A S JOHNSON, "WHEN A MAN is tired of London, he is tired of life." I was tired of both. Steve and Sung-ha flew to Spain and sang in competition, then returned in matching leather pants and bespoke berets, all fashioned for a trifle by a chain-smoking Barcelonian.

Their happy chatter brought to mind Guinevere, whose foibles were much missed: her subsistence on *café au lait* and cigarettes; her black market currencies of foot massage and tips; her late-night *Dr. Who* marathons; spooning; chess; the way she dreamed of wearing heels, but could not bear the pain; her worries about her weight, which turned out to be code for "I have boobies"; the way she meditated daily for half an hour, then slept for two; loved people, yet called babies *rug rats*; wore fur, petitioned for animal rights, ate only vegetables, and once a year sat down to a plateful of liver and onions.

I telephoned the Guest House Happy from a stall in Brixton Market. The pay phone made a dreadful clanking sound while we talked, as if Tolkien's dwarves were hammering nails into the coffin of our love. She was doing well, made thirty dollars an hour going TESOL, and loved Japan. But she missed me.

I told her London was like living in a novel. I did not say its name — *Nineteen Eighty-Four* — but from my tone she guessed it was a tale set in Hell. "Why don't you come to Japan?" she said. "You could go TESOL."

But I could not crawl back to her in defeat. I was on my way to Africa! And she already wore the pants; if I abandoned my own ship she'd also wear a sort of "I was right" captain's hat. I could not sanction that.

Yet if I stayed in London, I'd have to deal with Barney, Thatcher and the Queen. Samantha Fox was in there too, mostly working the night shift. I cursed the western Patriarchy, and vowed to leave for Africa that very week.

In the small ads at the back of *London: Time Out* I found a company called Lupus Travel that, under the *ægis* of a badly-drawn she-wolf, offered tickets at half the going rate. The office was under a stairway in Leicester Square. The agent was over-educated, and in BBC tones inquired my destination. I said, "Japan."

He frowned, collecting up his fee. "You understand it's illegal to land in Japan with a one-way ticket. If they check your papers at the airport, you'll be deported."

But I was thinking, *So that's why the tickets are half-price!* I'd deal with customs anon. When Sung-ha heard Guinevere and I were to be reunited, she cheered and clapped. No longer must she stifle love-cries while she and Stephen trysted quiet as mice on the bed, and I politely pretended to be asleep on the pull-out couch two yards away. When Nigel heard my plane flew *via* Moscow he brought warm beer and regaled me with tales of nuclear scientist *symposia* there.

"Æroflot™? No wonder the ticket's so cheap, they've got no safety standards, none! *Nada*! Zero! Zip! Planes drop out of the sky like plums!"

Stephen and Sung-ha rode the Tube with me to Heathrow. At Camden Circus we clambered down a stairwell that seemed to date from Roman times, and more recently had been used by soccer hooligans as an impromptu urinal. Above this reeking pit was hung a hasty poster:

SINCE YOU INSIST ON BEHAVING LIKE ANIMALS THE LAVATORY HAS BEEN CLOSED

The Æroflot™ desk thrummed with discord. Gorbachev had outlawed vodka just one year past, which rendered the present tense. An *apparatchik* stood at the luggage counter, rigid as a rusted clock, and downcast, as if he'd been shouted at by Barney for a month then turned to me with purple jowls that all but dripped cholesterol and grated, "What?!"

I showed my passport; he waved it aside and said the Heathrow handlers were on strike, so we must load our own *accoutrements*, as all the Soviet passengers had done. This incident was reported in the West as an example of state oppression, and in the East as one of team spirit.

At the gate I met Seamus: thin as a chimney sweep's brush, his head shaved on the sides, a rick of straw hair on top. His Irish passport showed a golden harp. I pulled out mine to find it gone. Seamus smirked as I fumbled faster and faster up and down my front, like a dentist fondling a patient before the æther wanes, but *Nada!* Zero! Zip!

I must locate it in the next ten minutes or my adventures would be over. Suddenly my mind flashed on an image of that small blue holy book, abandoned on the Æroflot™ luggage counter where the *apparatchik* had snarled at me. A voice within whispered *Run!*

I ran and ran till my popped knee throbbed, wobbled down hallways and up stalled escalators till trickles of sweat made slick the cushions of my *derrière*. I glimpsed in floor-to-ceiling glass what seemed to be a fat child from a nursery rhyme running directly at me, threw up my arms — and saw it was myself! Just twenty-five, I suddenly felt old.

At Æroflot™ my passport lay unnoticed on the counter where I'd left it, looking exactly as it had in my vision. No time to ponder this miracle; I flung me retrograde along those selfsame corridors, thinking on programs of exercise and dietary plans, and reached the gate just as the crew embarked. Panting, my face red as a gimbler's scrub, I plunked down beside Seamus and the plane clambered steeply into the arctic night.

CHAPTER XXVI.

THE GETTING OF WISDOM

*Red-eye to Russia — Laughter &
Forgetting — Gorbachev & Reagan —
The Number of the Beast*

G ETTING ANY INFORMATION at all about what
lay behind the Iron Curtain was next to impossible in those days. I'd never met a Russian, or even seen
one on TV; now I was surrounded by the Enemy, and it
filled me with alarm to note how human they seemed.
A sign blinked overhead:

NO SMOKING! FASTEN YOUR SEAT BELT!

The Voice had changed its tone again. Imagine!
shouting at a paying customer that way!

Moscow lay but two hours east across the Baltic, yet
Æroflot™ felt compelled to feed us. A florid woman
shoved a silver tray at me. On it, carefully washed, sat
yellow apples, bruised and past their prime. "Please!"
she said, as forcefully as the overhead sign. I bit: the
flesh was crystallized and soft. But the care with which
the fruit had been presented recalled to me a passage
from Kundera:

> Human beings have always aspired to an idyll, to that
> garden where nightingales sing, to that realm of har-
> mony where the world does not rise up as a stranger

against man and man against other men, but rather where the world and all men are shaped from one and the same matter.

Such Edenic imagery also permeates Marx, who saw history as a Hegelian tale of expulsion, exile and return: banished from the garden of tribal communal-

ism, then frog-marched through the wilderness of capitalism's nation-states, humanity would return at last to a worldwide worker's paradise. Gorbachev, a true $B_4L_1E_1E_1V_3E_1R_2$ in Marx's plan, saw *glasnost* and vodka-banning as tools used to repatriate humanity to this lost garden of the golden past. Conversely Reagan saw a future where America shone like a city on a hill: the New Jerusalem — an image cribbed from his mother's millennialist lay sermons. Small wonder their Iceland summit failed: the two could not see eye to eye, for each was drawn in opposite directions.

But I knew naught of politics. Even when setting

tableware I cannot consistently tell Left from Right. I only knew both men fit the description of the Antichrist in the Book of Revelation, for Mikhail Gorbachev bore on his brow the Mark of the Beast, while Ronald Wilson Reagan's name had Its Number encoded in a tally of the letters:

```
1 2 3 4 5 6
R O N A L D = 6
W I L S O N = 6
R E A G A N = 6
```

Thus did I while the air-time scribbling on Æroflot™ napkins till suddenly the jet lurched leeward, its ailerons rattled like collapsing scaffold, and Seamus woke and wailed in drunken terror. The pilot (furloughed perhaps from flying sorties in Kabul) barked something desperate and blurred from the cockpit; then down we spun like a sycamore seed into the whorling eye of the Evil Empire.

We flew so low over Moscow I could count chimney pots. I had imagined a landscape of concrete Stalin-era bunkers becalmed in fog, but saw instead the black slate roofs of ornate tenements, lit by the tall yellow slits of a thousand windows, and wrought-iron streetlamps that cast pools of light across crumpled ice heaped on the cobbled pavement. It was a scenery alien to me — not for its architecture, but for its lack of advertisement.

Seamus claimed there was a hostel where we might sleep *gratis*. I did not know this Irishman, but won't judge a man until I've walked a mile in his shoddy moccasins. Besides, the Irish are my Celtic cousins. Their ballyhooed proclivity for nail-bombs stems from an inborn otherness. They are not Anti-Christ, but they are anti-everything-else. While the Scots toiled to build the Future, like worker ants on amphetamines, the Irish excelled at doing nothing — which I intend as compliment. Considertheplightofwrittenwords:boggeddownuntilthe SeventhCenturywhentheIrish invented the space between them. Who would have thought adding nothing would render such benefit? Only the Irish.

This Celtic Otherness is manifest in every Irish thing, from great poverty to the great anti-novels of Joyce, Beckett and O Brien; and Seamus was the very model of a modern Irish degenerate. Every aspect of his hair and makeup whispered *Free!* — or at least, *Cheap!* Thus I entrusted myself to his money-saving intuitions as we searched for food, drink, and shelter from the freezing Russian night.

CHAPTER XXVII.

PROVIDING NOURISHMENT

The madness of the Five Year Plan — The
madness of my own plan — An interrupted
journey — Totalitarian by nature

R EAGAN AT LEAST PROVIDED NOURISHMENT
to his people while Moscow's stores sat empty as
a Welshman's threat. Even the restaurants seemed
dark as the depths of the Baltic, with few patrons at
dim tables. The grocery tills were monstrous clanking
things that gobbled sterling, dollars and yen but left
untouched the rubles foisted on us at customs. While
the West's free markets had made obesity a bigger
threat than hunger the East's planned economies left
their currencies soft as the small grey soap bars doled
out by the State's ubiquitous lavatory attendants.

At the hostel door a woman grimmer than three
prison guards relieved us of our shoes, as if we might
try to hang ourselves with the laces. I soon learned
why: we lay on couches set by the glowing hearth of an
enormous TV, upon whose snowy screen an ancient
general, weighed down by a giant khaki halo of army
hat, ground on and on about the Twelfth Five-Year
Plan.

To brainwash me takes but a quick rinse; and that
old soldier, droning his boneless speech, devoid of

consonants, that rasped like the slippers of a mental patient shuffling down a hallway, soon had me ready to agree to anything.

I redeemed my shoes and found Seamus smoking in the lobby. At one of the clanking tills I purchased a bottle of *Bodka* for thirty pence. We downed this misspelled sauce in a narrow place where chairs were stored. Thus warmed, I apprised Seamus of my one-way ticket, and my plan to breach Narita's walls by subterfuge. *Bodka* shot down his nose. He cried: "Narita's the biggest f____ ing fortress on the planet!"

I was aware. I'd seen the army tanks on my workymoon, and learned that in constructing the great ærodrome the State expropriated land that some had farmed a thousand years. The dispossessed, aided by Zenkyoto, a radical group of student activists, built of themselves a human pyramid to block the runway, while others attacked the control tower with homemade bombs. A decade on, Narita was still ringed by tanks. But I had a plan.

Replaned, we rocketed above Siberia. Night had fallen, or day not risen — I'd lost track. Below strung lights that might line gardened streets, or fence an endless *gulag*. Our craft seemed stuck in mid-air. Hours passed, and I recalled a night on Redfern Street when our neighbour Ralph — a carpenter who fashioned high-end furniture from exotic woods like butternut and bubinga — invited us for drinks. His wife drank *schnapps* and fell behind the couch, while their pretty and garrulous daughter dragged out a long strange yarn from behind the Iron Curtain.

Four of her friends had secured passage on the Trans-Orient Express. Upon reaching the steppes their locomotive stopped at a tiny railway station, and from their compartment the travelers saw a sign:

CHOCOLATE ICE CREAM

They ran across the platform, forgetting even their coats; bought cones; then hastened back to the train to find it gone. The Station Master at once grew fearful, and herded them into separate cells, each with only a bench and small, high window. The girl who told my neighbour this tale sat shivering for hours, then the Station Master entered with a glass of water and a pill and brow-beat her until she swallowed both. At once she felt unusual: soon she fell down on the bench and slept.

She woke frozen and terrified. By standing on the bench she glimpsed through the high window a thin grey road along which crept four Black Marias. She was bundled into one, beside a man in a fur *ushanka,* who swaddled her in sable but said not a word. They drove for hours through forests, fields, villages and towns to a great city: Moscow!

The girl's Maria stopped at a luxury hotel. There she was reunited with her friends, ate caviar and fruit, and was taken to the ballet. Next morning the four were returned to that remote station; the train arrived and in a compartment that seemed uncannily like yesterday's but was not, they found their luggage, crumpled clothes now freshly laundered. They surmised that their evening of forced ballet was meant to discredit any claims they might make of mistreatment. More likely, the Station Master's panic set in motion a train of bureaucratic incompetences that, combined with the same eager generosity that led the Soviets to force their Worker's Paradise on the world, resulted in this irrational scenario — just as their Five Year Plans led their economy to produce more left shoes than right, and ship them to Kamchatka and back by train for accounting purposes. None dared question the madness for, as Kundera concludes:

> There, everyone is a note in a sublime Bach fugue, and anyone who refuses to be one is a mere ... black dot that need only be caught and crushed between thumb and finger like a flea.

As our plane traversed the fjordic coast of North Korea I put my own mad plan into effect. I locked the toilet, shaved, bathed, and donned Hugh's pinstripe pants and magic wasitcoat, supposing that since the Japanese loved a businessman they might not check this one's ticket. I only had to $B_4L_1E_1E_1V_3E_1$ I was such and they would too.

Seamus scowled at my transformation. He had anticipated hi-jinks at Narita; now that entertainment was in doubt. The engines whetted pitch; we fell through bands of cloud and saw Japan laid out in grey and brown: roads, wires and wintery rice fields. I felt a swoon come on, as I had striding under the hot lights of Gary's stage; for in London I'd worn holes in the seat of those fine trousers, through which I could feel the scratchy fabric of the æroplane's upholstery.

CHAPTER XXVIII

GREATNESS

Narita — I try to hide the hole in my pants from the Authorities — Guinevere — The Guest House Happy

A T NARITA THE SUDDEN GREATNESS OF Japan seemed to hover in the icy air itself. While Heathrow's lazy Brits had let the moving walkways do the work pedestrians here used them to add velocity to their day. We swept down freezing ramps marked *gai-jin* — translated "alien", but literally, "not one of us." I struck up conversation with seven Russian diplomats who, thanks to that classless culture, had traveled steerage. Bespectacled customs agents herded all the suits aside and took our passports while Seamus and others traveling low were shunted behind a wall of bulletproof glass and searched down to their shaving kits.

When I breezed past with the *attachés* Seamus glanced up with sudden comprehension, and for a dangled moment I feared he would unmask me like a Bodysnatcher. Then he grinned: *F__k, yes!* and I was gone like a bad investment, chatting with a diplomat as if we were old chums. He said, "You are American."

"Canadian," I said.

"Well, you better put on your coat. Tokyo is cold in wintertime." He tried to help me on with mine; but I

had hung it behind me on my arm, the way a gentleman in Dickens might bustle up his coattails, trying to
cover the *lacuna* in my seat.

"Not as cold as Canada," I said, and slyly watched
an agent snap a rubber band 'round our eight passports, then hand them through the window of a booth.
That *snap!* rang sweet as harp strings — one step
closer — but the diplomat, still harping on the cold,
now seized my coat and with a Stalinist resolve tried
to force me into it. A nightmare vaudeville act ensued

that recalled Steve and Sung-ha buying flowers at
Camden Green while drunk. The Russian and myself
tugged back and forth, while from the customs booth a
visa stamp hammered down three, five, seven times —
a pause — the agent glanced up, saw my magic waistcoat, and — *chunk!*

I changed my trousers in a water closet and rode the
subway — its tunnels redolent with snow and vegeta-

tion, the very inverse of the reeky London Tube — to Tokyo, while all around the masses bowed and smiled, drank hot milkshakes and iced coffee from clattering machines, and read magazines back-to-front. I spent my last Cycloptic funds on the night bus to Kyoto, whereon I drowsed in a seat reclined almost into a bed, in slippers and a cotton *yukata* robe furnished by the bus line, and felt I'd slipped through not a border but a looking-glass.

The Guest House door slid sideways to reveal

Guinevere's lovely feet, and then the lovely rest of her. Hayashi, five feet tall, seized me in a bear hug and lifted me off the ground. "I need your help to get the small — sticky — fuzzy — white — *things* off of the carpet," he said, imagining I was here to work at minimum wage. I told him my new plan: to seek employ in the TESOL sector.

More had changed than just my pants. Jack and

Jane had gone to Hong Kong and left the place full of
Yanks: Jocelyn, tiny as a Skipper doll, whose entire
will was bent on finding food, like a hummingbird that
must consume its mass each day, or die; Erik, a writer,
who worked at a club on the fortieth floor of an Osaka
skyscraper where he lounged, played backgammon,
and lent the place a cosmopolitan air; Barry, short as
February, had thick bifocals and a gentle heart, into
which was jammed all the sybaritic passion of a full-
sized Yankee male; Bill was handsome as a model, and
moonlighted as such; Greg was both a stand up guy
and stand-up guy. Canadians Kris and Jeff both had
degrees in film, though Kris's real talent was catching
tossed chocolates in his mouth. He never missed! Jeff
had a detached smile, a Japanese girlfriend named
Hiroko, and a sebaceous cyst behind his ear. While
he stanched the puss Hiroko brought coffee and knelt
adjacent. "I rike your penis," she said, as though she'd
been taught this by the others in cruel jest.

I shook my head: "No! No! You *like* my penis." For
clearly this was a ruse designed to shock: no normal
Japanese girl lives among *gaijin*. She laughed with
glee, and thenceforth called me "Dad" — an omen I
ignored till now.

CHAPTER XXIX

THE ABYSS

A waking dream — Into the Abyss —
Mysterium Tremendum — Erik lends me
a book

M Y WIFE SWAM DEEP IN THE ABYSS of dreams,
sometimes while she was still awake, as on that
first night when I slept jet-lagged in her arms. She bade
me assist her in the construction of a wall of invisible
matchboxes which she hoped would divert a column of
turtles that was wending its way across the *tatami* mats
into her closet and living among her shoes. It gave me
joy to watch her noctambulistic toil, and listen to her
muttered dispatches from inside a dream.

But when I fell into sleep I was dragged down into
a primæval ocean where half-formed creatures feed
upon each other, biting and sucking and snapping
their teeth in the murk. Along the silty sea bed flounces
a Japanese *salaryman* — a businessman complete with
briefcase — who charges me like a hungry eel, then
draws back in horror. His jaws distend like an angler
fish; he wobbles towards me so that I can see leeches
and limpets clamped to his suit sleeves, neck and face.
They eat his blood and poop it out, and he must dine
on these excretions. Then comes a dreadful roar, and
from the dimness I see some vast *thing* advances:

This vision so unhinged me that I rose, and found it was already dawn, or dusk: the light was changing. In the kitchen Erik toasted *pano mimi* — "ears of bread" — the heels of loafs that locals fed to pets, and *gaijin* used as crude delivery systems for Familiar Cheese. Jocyelyn ate bagfuls of the stuff at no great price, for it cost ten cents a heap.

I told Erik my dream; he crunched, and thought awhile, then gave me a scuffed paperback — *The Anat-*

omy of Dependence — by a Japanese psychiatrist named Takeo Doi. Victoria, who'd come from New York to study culinary arts, claimed it was the key to understanding Japan. Indeed, it said so on the cover.

I read for hours while other *gaijin* stirred and shuffled down the hall towards the full-open cock. Doi studied in post-War California, where he grew perplexed by the tyranny of choices, for at dinner he was asked if he would like a drink. His host's apparent rudeness shocked him. In Japan a host intuits his guest's needs and fills them before they can arise. At dessert Doi found he must choose again: tea or coffee? Milk or sugar? A cigarette? A new constitution? For Doi these constant choices rang of cold indifference, though he knew this was the opposite of his hosts' intent.

Returned to Tokyo, he noted Japanese psychiatrists wrote their diagnoses in German, discarding anything that would not fit into that procrustean frame, including problems of *attachment* that might be far more easily described by using the common Japanese term *amæ*.

Born of a child's first word — *uma-uma,* a plea for breast milk — *amæ* describes the happy sense of enfolding oneself in a mother's unconditional love. In Japan every human bond is expressed in terms of that *Ur-*attachment. In fact, they have more words for such than Scots for rain: *amæ, amæi, amanzuru* — yet there is no single word for the concept in English. The closest are clumsy technical terms, like Freud's "primary object-choice" or the "passive-object love" written of by Balint (who also notes that no European tongue distinguishes between active and passive love). Conversely, *amæ* describes "a positive attitude towards the spirit of dependence" — the very inverse of our Western declarations of independence.

This struck me also as the nub of *zen*, whose monks seek to break the Wall 'twixt man and Nature; to be reabsorbed into the world, as if into the arms of some Mother Goddess. Guest House alumnus Hans, a student of *zen*, disagreed. He said the point was to sever attachment to the world of physical sensation: to let go of everthing, and resolve oneself to nothing. Like Seamus, Hans was skilled at doing nothing. Unlike that Irishman he made a hundred dollars a day, by standing downtown in silent vigil wearing a monk's robe and shoes with no socks, in cold weather. *Salarymen* startled by this sockless *gaijin's* piety cast thousand-yen notes into his wicker begging bowl; then he would thaw in the adjacent McDonald's™ with hot coffee and cheap Korean cigarettes that tasted of soap.

Intrigued, I joined Hans in *zazen* meditation at the nearby temple. We sat on flat pillows beneath a painted wooden buddha. The little old monk who played the part of *sensai* opened the temple doors wide, that we might in silence contemplate the beautiful garden: rocks; trees; and also snow, which drifted in and settled near my foot.

CHAPTER XXX.

ATTACHMENT

Amæ theory of attachment — Einstein vs.
Bohr — Schrodinger & his Cat

S O I ABANDONED MY ATTACHMENT to the cold.
The monk rang a bell; the note died slowly, and in
the silence that remained my inner Voice roared like
a breaking wave, then ebbed to a distant line of ques-
tioning. Soon I felt nothing, except a throbbing in my
knee, wound up beneath me in a fleshy pretzel. I tried
to let go of the pain but it clung to me like a baby and
screamed until I began to fidget — and this fidgeting
was sin!

The monk fetched a big flat stick from under the
Buddha and stood behind me like Casey at the Bat. If
I moved again, he'd "let me have it"; and I must thank
him — *arigato, sensai* — but instead imagined punching his small wrinkled face; and then the police would
come and I would go to jail because I'd left my *gaijin*
card at the Guest House . . .

Three hours later I hobbled home, grim as a peasant mugged by God, and later saw that monk schlep a
vacuum cleaner to his Porsche. Paul nodded. "He's
loaded. At New Year he makes a thousand dollars an
hour chanting *sutras* at houses. He doesn't even have to

go, he sends a student. He can send up to ten students to ten different houses!"

Enlightenment by proxy franchise? So much for *zen* detachment. In any case, why suffer to see the light when science has proved that light itself is a bewildering paradox, a wave and particle both? How could that be? It made no rational sense, like saying a man is good and evil.

Then to my dismay I learned some wonky German wag named Schrödinger had proved this possible, by mathematical equation! Not only that: he'd fleshed the idea out using his Cat. The Cat's more famous than the equation, for it appears thus:

while the equation looks like this:

$$[\frac{-\hbar^2}{2m}\nabla^2+V]\Psi=i\hbar\frac{\partial}{\partial t}\Psi$$

Back to the Cat. Suppose we put that wretched creature in a soundproof box, along with a hand grenade that has a ten-second fuse. (Fear not! It's army surplus: there's a fifty-fifty chance it won't go off.) Ten seconds later we hold the following truths to be self-evident: 1. Because the box is soundproof, we cannot know if the grenade went off or not unless we open it and look. 2. Schrodinger was a monster.

But is his Cat alive, or dead? It can't be both. All we need do is open the box and look — but hold! According to Schrödinger's equation the Cat is both alive *and* dead. It's in an *eigenstate*: a super-state, where two opposing worlds coexist simultaneously. It only becomes one of these things when we open the box and look. It's our act of observation, of measurement, that causes one of these worlds to manifest and the other to collapse.

ERWIN SCHRÖDINGER: CAT KILLER?

Now, a cat in a box is one thing and a subatomic particle quite another. As with Austrian economics, the magic is in the math. But in my cheeerful way I fancied that by force of will I might choose between possible worlds and thereby create my own reality. I pictured a better job, better home, better health — and in a fortnight was hired to go TESOL at Guinevere's school: three thousand dollars' salary, plus benefits! The contract stipulated I must never disgrace the company "by action or by thought." What of it? Gimbling was here no crime! I told them my diploma was in the mail, and signed.

At Christmastime a businesman I'd befriended became enamoured of Guinevere's dulcet voice and asked her to record a series of tapes instructing *sala-rymen* in "bedroom English", that they might find love abroad, or at least a broad. Guinevere scoffed and flushed; he, to make amends, offered to rent us a friend's house in Seiwadai, a mountain village near Kobe, quiet as a temple, its streets lined with cherry blossom trees. The house had two pianos and a garden. The street address was 666 — so I'd play the Beast. What of it? We said farewell to the Guest House crew and moved in on a freezing January day.

Then, tilting at the windmill of health, I joined a nearby club where each noon scores of housewives smashed *kendo* sticks together with a tremendous "*HA!*" while *salarymen* ran round the rooftop track. But here I hit a Wall. For I am centred in my head (some would say trapped), and drive my body like a forklift. Exercise is agony to me!

But I was so determined, I was predetermined. I pumped so much iron I knew the words of pop tunes blaring from the PA:

Touch me! Touch me! I wanna feel your body!

And was astounded to learn the chanteuse was Samantha Fox! She had metastasized from Page Three of the *Sun* to *Times* Spokeswoman to International Pop Star. She had created her own reality. Clearly she knew something of Schrödinger's Cat.

CHAPTER XXXI.

INFLUENCE

Adulthood Day — Jack & Jane — An
open sewer — We arrive too late to party

INFLUENCED BOTH BY Schrödinger's equation and Doi's *amæ* theory (Sam Fox was in there too, wearing divers gimbling chaps) I saw Japan, and my whole life, in strange new light. And it was good. My marriage prospered. In Seiwadai Guinevere and I had at last world enough, and time. On Saturdays Erik arrived by Hanyku^{TM} train and we played guitar, wrote comedy sketches and laughed till dawn. His humour ran deep as Jack's, yet was more gentle. "Let's talk about your bonus," he'd say, shaking his head.

I wondered how this budding bromance would sit with Jack, who hated all things American, from light beer to Reagan. He and Jane were now returned from Hong Kong. By phone we set a double date in Nara, the ancient capital, on the night of the Fire Festival, which Guinevere and I had seen on our w'moon: Tall grass on the hill above Kofuku-ji temple was set ablaze; monks leaped through flame while thousands drank beer and flooded up the ancient steps towards that conflagration, chanting.

Superposed upon this was Adulthood Day, when

girls who will turn twenty that year don silk kimonos and rice-straw sandals in a style so ancient and complex that specialists must enrobe them and put up their hair, then stand in giggling groups of two and three under paper umbrellas, framed by bamboo, pretty as a Hokusai print. Jack said it was a dying tradition: it cost thousands to prepare, and most girls now opted for a car instead.

KOFUKU-JI TEMPLE WITH OPEN SEWER

At Todai-ji, Guinevere wept to see the giant bronze Buddha. I noted the stillness of the temple pond. "You haven't seen it in summer," said Jack. "It *seethes* with turtles. It's an open sewer."

We dined at a *robatayaki* near the temple, chuckling at the admixture of fire and alcohol. Hayashi lived in fear his *gaijin* friends would set the Guest House ablaze through lack of respect for fire. We scoffed, until Kris hung his shirt above the kerosene heater in the common room and slipped away to brush his teeth while it dried. Yukio, the maid, entered the empty room to find that demon shirt flailing its arms in a column of fire. The next day Hayashi held up the shirt, burnt at the edges like a pirate map. "I only say it once," he said. "Fire: no joke."

And yet tonight crowds drunk as suburban housewives would swing buckets of the stuff through dry grass around the biggest wooden temple in the world! For Jack this smacked of a schizophrenia more profound than the labels on Canadian shampoo. He feared the dreadful Bomb had split not just the atom, but the Japanese soul. I talked of Schrödinger's Cat: perhaps their double standards were not *schizoid* but *simultaneous*. We quarrelled about atoms until the womenfolk begged, "Come *on!* We're *late!*"

We rushed outside and joined the crowd to find it gone. The hill was burnt to ash. *Damn!*

That month I started "work" — lunch twice a week with Takahashi, who toiled at a starch factory. For days I worried about him schlepping sacks of starch onto a forklift's tines to pay my fee; but one lunch hour he said he'd narrowly convinced his father not to build a helicopter pad on the factory roof. I asked him what he did at the starch factory.

"I own," he said. "I'm sorry." For he was simultaneously rich and humble. Conversely, the most abject Japanese soul seemed bolstered by an inner strength. On a road island in Umeda, in the heart of Osaka, in the shadow of an elevated highway, there lived a man with nothing but the clothes upon his back — plus self-respect! At dawn he swept his island clean of cigarette butts, folded away his bed and sat erect as a monk upon the kerbstone with a keg of beer from a nearby vending machine. At dusk he slept on cardboard while *salarymen* streamed through his bedroom. It must take dedication to remain so poor in a land where having lunch can earn a man a house with two pianos.

Takahachi soon mastered every common English word save *no*. He practised, but could not put it *into* practice. "See you next week," I said. "Yes," he said. "But next week is difficult, because I am in Thailand." I nodded. "In two weeks, then."

"Yes! Yes! But — but —"

". . . but you'll still be in Thailand?"

"YES!" he said, relieved. "YES! YES! !"

It was a jigsaw moment. In a flash I saw why Japan appeared so strange: they said YES! to opposites — spirit and matter, future and past, flammable and inflammable. Even their word for *no* was YES! It was a great leap forward; meanwhile, back at the Guest House Happy, Jack was depressed. He'd read in the *Japan Times* that Reagan believed in the biblical prophecy of Armageddon. "We're screwed!" he said.

I thought: I'll tell him about saying YES! Perhaps he can say YES! to Reagan. So I met him and Jeff at a bar downtown, and we quarreled about atoms until we missed the last train home: we were trapped in the futuristic wasteland of Umeda for the night's duration.

CHAPTER XXXII.

THE DURATION

*A rainy night — A gimbler's paradise — I
get into a fight — Living on the street*

X-RATED CLUBS RINGED the station just as tanks had ringed Narita. There issued the ancient oracle of THUNDER ABOVE as rain set in; THUNDER BELOW as the station's metal doors crashed down like rolltop desks. A billboard advertised rooms in an adjacent capsule hotel. These would be Spartan — TV, air conditioner and bed, as if we were become Spam™ for a night — but dry, and cheap.

We three sloshed Spamwards through ankle-deep monsoon. Jack kicked a pile of rubbish outside a shuttered *ramen* shop and chuckled with glee as rats streamed from it and vanished down an open sewer. "Say YES! to rats!" he said.

We crossed the road island where the proud street bum lay fast asleep. Jack said, "Say YES! to concrete!" I saw his point. The man's fate seemed more terrible at night in this landscape cobbled from *Blade Runner* sets: noodle shops steamed, trains rattled overhead and giant electric billboards flashed

I FEEL COKE™

into the thundery sky. I felt a need for beer before resigning to my Spammy fate. We dried our socks in a bar so small the front and back walls seemed to touch. Jeff practised his Japanese on an aged *geisha* whose lipstick had quite missed her mouth and covered half her chin. Jack pointed at the food cooler. "Watch: you'll see cockroaches press their bellies against the glass."

It was the week of Examination Hell, when schoolchildren sit their college entrance exams. The results would determine their whole lives. The stress was such that suicide spiked; Jack claimed five kids had leaped from their schoolhouse roof, holding hands.

Outside again, the rain was worse. We strolled like *flaneurs* through an arcade full of sex clubs. Women in nurse costumes beckoned us with fans. Within, anything was permitted, for God was not just dead, but had never been. Pleasure was all! A man might spank unruly schoolgirls or be diapered by a nun. I wondered aloud if they had overnight rooms.

Jeff meanwhile leafed through a magazine dedicated to the coprophilic lifestyle. On the cover a corseted trollop shat in a man's mouth. Dear non-existent God! Compared to that poor swine's fate, gimbling seemed a gentleman's pursuit.

Jack sputtered like the kettle that invented steam power. "Sick! Sick! Sick!" It backed me to the Wall like a beast. Confusing as such strange languages of desire might seem, I could not ask clemency for gimbling while condemning these poor cousins. I felt I must take a stand — and yet, with love. What Jack needed was a hug. I'd force *ama* upon him! YES! I grabbed him in a bear hug big as Hayashi's. Jeff joined in too. (He later said he'd thought it was a *group hug* situation; in fact we had enjoyed completely different evenings, simultaneously superimposed on that same thundrous night.) Jack tried to wriggle free, and my attempt to impose *amæ* went awry as I locked his head under my gym-beefed arm.

How scrawny his Gumby™ neck! YES! What power rushed up my spine! YES! I'd never felt so alive, and YES! Jack wrestled loose, chuckled nervously, and suddenly put his thumbs over my eyes like Rutger Hauer in *Blade Runner.* But *I* was playing the part of Hauer tonight — wasn't Jack the Good Man? I let the rain run down my neck for a long beat. Jack drops his thumbs. I grin a grin I show to none: the gimbler's rictus, the face of the Irrational:

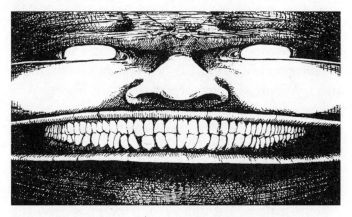

Jack blanches with terror and flees wailing into the warren of alleyways, lost. But I have tarried on these streets, in gimbling parlours, cinemas and magazine stands, and know the lay. I run along an alley and wait for my friend behind a wall; and when he stumbles past I leap out with a great "*HA!*" louder than forty housewives smashing *kendo* sticks. Jack runs like mascara in the rain, fading, gone. Jeff follows for a block, then shouts after him, "I have my pride!" and shuffles back to me.

I've no idea what he means in his alternate evening. We wend through rain that falls so hard it ricochets back up like bullets, until we come once more to the road island of the proud bum. I stare at his shock of hair. I feel abject as he: I'd put my best friend in a headlock, and enjoyed it!

Then comes another jigsaw moment: YES! *I see!* The road island is no metaphor, but concrete — the only spot for miles above the waterline in rain like this. The elevated roadway is his roof. He's not mad but only poor. It should be no crime.

As I stand struck, the man awakes. He gazes up at me for a long moment then thrusts out a grubby hand. We shake. He moves aside to make room. I can't refuse my host: that's not *amæ*. So I say YES! to concrete and lie down. My heart pounds on the pavement. We are soft creatures in this stony world. Why not be gentle with each other?

We three lie drunk on cardboard, staring up at the great concrete vault of modernity's cathedral. Jeff practices his Japanese on our host. He takes the language barrier seriously.

That was the last time I saw Jack. And who can blame him? Should he say YES! to headlocks? To evil grins? But for the first time I'd stood my ground — my true ground, a potter's field of perversion, a gimbler's Golgotha — yet the world still *was*. And though I'd been in Asia for what Takahachi would call a *business quarter*, only now was I arrived in the Land of Wa.

AUTHOR / PUBLISHER
INTERFACE

SEVEN YEARS HAD PASSED since Rolf and I walked 'round the dog park talking about this book — yet still there was no progress. The problem lay in its dual nature: for in our specialized world suspicion falls on he who would illustrate his own writing, as these opposites are not supposed to touch.

Word and image are opposites in that, like particles and waves, an image is always one thing, while words by their nature must be more than one. Consider three men drinking at a *robayata* in Umeda: their bill is twenty-five hundred yen; each antes a thousand, and from this three thousand each takes a hundred, and between them leave the waiter two hundred for his tip. (They must be drunk. There is no tipping in Japan. But I digress). Thus each paid nine hundred — that's twenty-seven hundred — plus two hundred for the tip makes twenty-nine hundred. Where is the missing yen?

The problem springs from confusing the word *three* with the number 3 (which, like a drawing, is only ever one thing : 3.

In arithmetic the problem is no problem:

2,500 (bill) + 300 (change) + 200 (tip) = 3,000

But when expressed in words, it goes unnoticed that the narrator first counts up from zero then changes midstream to counting down from thirty. The "missing" yen fell into that blind spot, which is as necessary to language as it is to the eye. In fact, Wittgenstein reduced all philosophical dispute down to this blind spot.

But are not optical illusions, like the Duckrabbit, two things at once? Even Wittgenstein was tricked by this for a spell, and spent the first half of his career on a picture theory of language, only to abandon it with his *summa*, *Philosophical Investigations*, wherein he concludes the duckrabbit is a deviant: with words, context is all.

I wrestled with these ideas instead of writing until January then phoned Rolf to tell him things were look-

WHAT'S UP, DUCK?

ing up, which is what writers tell publishers when the money has run out. Instead of providing detail (for there was none) I waxed on the cyclical nature of the narrative, and how the story's last sentence was also the first.

Rolf said, "Like the book *Dhalgren*."

I was so startled I forgot to lie. In fact, I'd cribbed the conceit from *Finnegans Wake*, but sure enough, *Dhalgren* begins: *to wound the autumnal city* and ends 900 pages later with I *have come to*

Never having reached the story's end, I never knew it had none. Yet that broken sentence rang with *déjà vu*, for in expropriating the book's dual layouts I'd used page 806 as my model, whereon the sentence appears whole, halfway down the left ~~hemisphere~~ column. Strange coincidences abounded with that book.

"Look at the epigraph," Rolf said. I was ahead of him: "But is that our George Stanley?" He assured me it was; and as he spoke I noticed I'd written over the page numbers, turning them into palimpsests, for the paperback I'd grabbed at random to help me keep things straight with InDesign was the book *Dhalgren*.

A month later, deep in thought, I walked down the street where Snowden's Books sits empty, and glanced up just as the Google car drove past and shot me from the roof. The metaphor I'd constructed in my Preface — of standing like a ghost before a ghost — was now concrete. I knew not what to make of this Ouroborean clusterf__k around the book *Dhalgren*, but at that moment I thought, *At last! it can begin.*

My first draft took but three short months; in May Rolf came over from Vancouver and we parsed the manuscript for a day and a half, then my sister called with terrible news.

PART TWO

In
quantum
mechanics anything that
is not forbidden is
compulsory.

— MURRAY GELL-MANN

THE SHIP PASSED THROUGH THE TAIL OF A MONSOON.
SEE P. 177

CHAPTER XXXIII.

RETREAT

*I seek counsel — Amae revisited —
Amaterasu — Inlaws*

TWADDLE! I THOUGHT, IN FULL RETREAT from
my own ideas, entrained towards Seiwadai at
dawn. Succesful *amæ* strategies do not end with headlocks! Where was the harmony of chocolate pies?
There must be some detail of Doi's ideas I'd missed.
I resolved to read his little book again, fell into a *cantilevered* swoon, and slumbered till my train hit the
terminal buffers of the Hankyu™ line, high in the
hills. I crossed through cool air to the opposite track,
rode south, blacked out, and woke downtown back in
Umeda. I headed north again; slept eight stops past my
own; drowsed four stops south; north two; and by this
gradual accumulation of halves resolved old Xeno's
paradox by arriving home in time for breakfast.

Guinevere agreed I needed help, with the gimbling
and the Crab Thing and now the headlocks. In *Kansai Time Out* I found a company that promised pro-
fessional help at rock-bottom fees, so telephoned a
councillor in Kobe, a nice Australian bloke. I crawled
abed and dreamed he and myself were deep in conversation — except he was now a *sheila* with an English

accent and lived not in Kobe but in the top right corner of a seaside town that was somehow also a map of itself. We sat on her steps and gazed across a great harbour, where stood a brace of immense temple *torii,* red as a geisha's lips.

Next day the Aussie telephoned to say he'd caught flu, and I must go instead to a woman named Deirdre Putnam who lived along the coast near the Konan Women's University. I climbed to her house and sat on her steps to pluck up my nerve, and when I turned there came another jigsaw moment — *Hai!* — for in the bay below stood a brace of giant cargo derricks, each painted that distinctive *torii* red.

This so unmanned my rational defense that instead of telling Deirdre about Umeda I blurted out my real concern: I was a gimbler, and feared this would wreck my marriage and my life. She did not call the police (gimbling? What of it?) but asked if Guinevere could come next time. She saw no point in dealing with such issues outside of their context: relationship was all.

Guinevere read Jung voraciously but balked before analysis-as-deed, for she felt more comfortable with me cast in the part of *L'Etranger.* Yet she was nothing if not courageous, and so, warily, we tested our changing roles. The sessions bore much fruit — though I soon noted Deirdre seemed bent on reconciling us not to each other, but to our parents; and in July flew back to England to confront her own, who'd never given her the space she needed, hence her self-exile in the Land of Wa.

At a loose end, I delved deep into Doi, and as often happens, found that book was not just content but also context. For in my first reading I'd barely noticed the author's insistence that *amæ* was rooted in spiritual fields, its unconditional mother-love made manifest in Shinto's prime deity — the Sun-Goddess Amaterasu, who at the Dawn emerged from a cave, like Hume or Zarathustra, and birthed humanity. From her body was the Archipelago made: each island a limb, each bay a curve of thigh. Thus Amaterasu permeates all — yet even She is subject to the field of *amæ,* for Her name is derived from that word. Doi concludes by quoting D.T. Suzuki: "At the basis of the ways of thinking and feeling of the Westerner is the father. It is the mother that lies at the bottom of the Oriental nature".

In short, Doi claimed Japan, and the whole Orient, was a vast Matriarchy that flowed with the all-permeating tidal power of *amæ*.

AMATERASU EMERGING FROM HER CAVE

CHAPTER XXXIV.

POWER

Male and female — The Little Prince —
The big baby

YET NOWHERE WAS THIS POWER visible. Japan seemed matriarchal as a barbershop quartet. God might be treated as a woman, but actual women were treated as dogs. That year the sex trade imported a hundred thousand Filipino girls and kept them in kennels. Even grammar was complicit: I called my chopsticks *hashi*; Guinevere called hers *o-hashi* — honourable chopsticks — because of her low station. Lower than chopsticks? That is where I draw the line!

That week at a Kobe school chairs were pushed aside, and tables set with every kind of food — *okaino-mayaki, oden, natto*. The women stood spontaneously at the tables and served the men, who lounged on couches like little emperors. I sat beside the student presently known as Prince, perhaps for his pencil moustache, and asked if he was having fun.

"Yes," he said. "But I'm so hungry!"

"The food's right there!"

Prince shook his head. "The women have much —" he flipped through his Berlitz and found the word: *power*. I told him that was not the word he sought.

Prince checked his work: YES! *Power.*

He said he'd recently been hired at an electric company, which, as was their wont, worked new employees eighteen hours a day to burn away the dross of college life and leave naught save the essential *salaryman.* If he objected he'd become *madogiwa-zoku* — given a "desk by the window" and no work, ever again. His life would pass in *zen* contemplation of the view — and while the window was a metaphor; the view would be concrete. Exhausted, he had slept through lunch. And now his female classmates had shunned him for his "bad eye" — they said he'd looked on them with lust. "I can't help myself," he said.

He also couldn't feed himself with women present. It wasn't done. He might as soon shed his pants. I looked at the snack table again, but now I saw (or did I dream it?) the womenfolk had the food blockaded, shoulder to shoulder, a silky platoon that doled out treats to those deemed worthy. I began to wonder: was there another Japan, where women wore the pants, invisible to me, superposed upon the world I saw, like Schrödinger's *eigenstates?*

One evening I sat on the balcony with the director of Mino-o School: Tanaka, whose Elvis bouffant and huge spectacle frames overpowered his small kind face. He came from Shikoku. "Very natural, mostly forest," he said.

I asked about the litter problem. "No problem," he said. "There's nobody around so —" he mimed tossing a can under a bush. Thus as a child had he indulged *amæ* at the expense of Mother Earth. He'd just taught a class of boys, and almost fainted from the strain. Why so unruly? This too stemmed from *amæ.* "Japanese parents are afraid to discipline their children in case they don't like us anymore," he said. Tanaka lit a Mild Seven™ and enjoyed the smooth, rich taste in a way we no longer can then told a long, strange tale.

"In Japan, when you are little, you sleep in mother's bed, and she does e-e-everything for you," he said, stretching the vowel out like toffee. The end result: at college he had no idea how to feed himself. He dined on instant *ramen* for a year, succumbed to malnutrition and lay prostrate for ten days in his apartment, soiling his futon and hallucinating.

But then, a miracle! His mother dropped in for a surprise visit. She took him home and nursed him well; in three short months he learned to walk again. During this second infancy she hired a matchmaker, who found him a wife. In wedding photographs she and the bride's matchmaker sit at opposite ends of the table, like rooks in chess. Tanaka did not know his wife from Eve, and found they did not see eye to eye. What of it? He could eat again!

Now came *Sakura* — cherry blossom festival —— and all the trees went off at once, like mortars, showering petals on the crowd outside the station. Spring was returned, a conquering army. Outside the Kinkaku-ji Temple gate a little boy wept while his older brothers, ten and eight, laughing, propped up their grandfather. He was so drunk he lay across their backs facing the empty sky. But this was no disgrace: he was the patriarch of that clan, and as Doi writes, "The person who can embody infantile dependence in its purest form is most qualified to stand at the top of Japanese society". The Emperor must be "propped up" by his court, completely dependent on those around him. Indeed, the Japanese employ the selfsame conjugation when addressing emperors and infants.

Now I saw babies everywhere I looked: in Kurosawa's *One Wonderful Sunday* the heroine Masaeko laughs and calls her beau "a gigantic baby! The biggest baby in the world!" In Miyazaki's *Spirited Away* the biggest baby in the world is no metaphor but concrete. The heroine, Sen, is lost in a dreamworld dominated by the crone Yubaba. Yet Yubaba herself is at the mercy of her gigantic baby boy, Boh. In the penultimate scene Yubaba sets Sen a task: she must find her parents in a herd of swine. Boh warns his mother, "If you make Sen cry, I won't like you any more." And the old witch, who runs that dreamworld in the style of Stalin, *trembles!*

BOH, THE GIGANTIC BABY

CHAPTER XXXV

PROGRESS

*The public & private — 46 Ronin —
The Little Emperor System — Midori —
Guilt & shame*

T HUS I PROGRESSED through Doi's book compar-
ing what he wrote to what I saw around me, and
with gathering momentum began to grasp not only
Japan's culture, but hidden elements of my own.

The crux: because the bond between mother and
child was unbreakable here, the counry's smallest
denomination was two. There was no such thing as
a private citizen. Their word for "private" — *uchi* —
means "inner circle", and has naught to do with soli-
tude. And because the tree's roots do not reach down
to the individual level, its branches cannot reach up
to include th'entire sky. Their word for "public" —
oyake — refers not to everyone, but only to members
of Japan's biggest and oldest clan, the Emperor's family, the Tokugawas, which through its power has long
imposed its will on all the smaller cliques. This has
vast consequence.

Consider Japan's most cherished national tale, *Forty
Seven Ronin:* the *samurai* Oishi, who must avenge his
Lord Asano's death, compares his task holding the
company together now that their master is gone to

that of the iron ring that bands together the slats of a wooden *furo* hot tub. This is the history of Japanese politics in a nub. We imagine they enjoy an almost disturbing national cohesion. Such does exist, but not as the result of natural proclivity: it counterbalances their natural proclivity to split into clans.

The result of this, writes Doi, is "Little Emperors everywhere." I saw this all around: my private student, Takahachi, was such. He'd recently returned from Thailand, where he ate tiger with the king. "Tastes very bad!" he said, giggling *sans* guilt at his own villainy. After supper the men sent their wives shopping, then slept like babes. Sleep is the currency of the super-rich.

While he'd been gone my company, ECC, had sent me as a visiting instructor to schools all over the Kansai region. Each seemed a different clan, and each director a different style of Little Emperor.

The Emperor of Mino-o School, my friend Tanaka, smoked like a soggy campfire and gazed out of a window while his two secretaries did all the work. The classrooms were dark, for the school lay along an alley that opened on a little garden filled with baby statues — shrines to aborted children where women laid a pebble for each infant lost to science. Despite Japan's reverence for babies, abortions now outnumbered births. Experts blamed privation after the war. Tax breaks were offered; still the birth rates plunged.

The Emperor of Takarazuka School, Chano, wore leather driving gloves, enjoyed sport-shooting and took great interest in his charges. The place was bright and hot, adjacent to a famous private "cram" school full of children who had no life save study. Sometimes in class they laid their heads down on their desks and slept.

Kobe School stood above the harbour, hot and muggy, beside a scorching welder's shop where millions of car parts, bolts, gaskets and metal fittings were hoisted into a cavernous vault. The Emperor, Yoshi, was a shadow character, small and bald, who never talked to *gaijin* but sent his Number Two to do his dirty work. Everyone hated this Number Two, though Yoshi could clearly be seen at his desk in the corner, pulling the strings. His subterfuge made Kobe the most dangerous of the schools, save only Toyonaka, where taught the lovely Midori.

Tiny in three-inch heels, Midori was no Lolita, but mirrored the *kansai* landscape: flat at lower altitudes and mountainous higher up, she clacked through classrooms wearing insensible shoes, her long black ponytail a-swing. "Every guy in the office has a thing for her," said Trigg, a sporty Yank who'd sweated through his button-down, and not just from the heat. I was unconcerned. I had a wife. Suddenly Midori sat beside me and opened Freud's *Jokes and Their Relation to the Unconscious.* Her skin was cream stirred into coffee. Now damp as Trigg, who twonked "Candyman" nearby on the school guitar, I felt my eyes roll helpless into her *décolletage,* and there glimpsed, clear and fleeting as semaphore flags upon a distant cliff (or did I dream it?) the tiny tell-tale tic-tac-toe marks left by a gimbling frame!

Had she no shame? In fact, she had no guilt, which Doi claims requires individuation. As the smallest denomination available in Japan is two — mother and child — guilt finds thin soil. Far more effective in the eyes of the group is shame.

Western guilt can only be expunged by a transcendent entity who can forgive all: God. But Japan has no such thing. Their gods exist beyond the pale of human woes like morality: they are forces of nature, like Godzilla, who is not good or evil, or even supernatural, but merely big.

Nor do they need such metaphysical clemency, for shame, rooted in the group, can be expunged by the same. Westerners too wrestle with this primal fear of shame, of ostracism from the group (Bonhoffer wrote that shame is born from our "helpless longing to return to unity with the Origin"). But against this we are forearmed by legends of the Fall: the expulsion from Eden. By starting our spiritual journey with separation, the Bible and its descendant texts — *Moses and Monotheism, et al.* — make it possible for us to endure our alienation from the Source. This has vast consequence.

For by surviving this separation we set in motion the rise of the Patriarchy, and also the need of a great Redemption at the End of Time, where Reagan's shining city on the hill awaits: the New Jerusalem. Hence the religious cast of the aphorism "Give me liberty or give me death." There is no other option: we must follow our path of exile through till the end. Conversely, Japanese like Midori have never left the garden and feel no guilt. Yet anything that sets them apart from the group is pain itself.

Later my friend Akio took me to the Selfish Coffee Bar, by which was meant "self-serve", though waiters rushed upon us. One dropped a tray; after the crash came silence. I said in Canada the patrons would have clapped; the guilty party might even take a bow. Akio nodded. "But in Japan, we feel shame."

CHAPTER XXXVI.

DARKENING OF THE LIGHT

The evolution of the Voice — Enjoy! —
Chomolongman — Maurice Wilson

H E THEREBY SHEWED THE DARKNESS of *amæ*: a total collapse of boundaries and reabsorption by the Great Mother would mean death; thus all attempts to *amæ* are ultimately doomed. In its unappeasable nature it resembles the Western "conscience", which we might picture brightly as Jiminy Cricket wishing upon a star, or darkly, as Norman Bates's dead mother — that chirping or harping inner voice that can never be assuaged.

This inner Voice began with Yahweh, who spake from thunder. Through the long story of the Jews this Voice became internalized by degree, till in the Book of Acts it descended from heaven, so that the entire community began to speak in tongues.

That babble was modulated into private dialogue by the Irish invention of the confessional booth, where it became the "still, small voice of the Holy Spirit"; then into an internal monologue when Luther rid us of said booth; and with the death of God became Freud's "superego": the Voice of the secular state. Thus, Reason first advanced in regions where the confessional was removed — foremost among them, Scotland and Holland.

I'd long noted how the confessional booth mirrors the twinned hemispheres of the brain: we sit in one dark half, aware of our sin, guilt separation from God; and from the other half issues a whispered Voice that brings absolution and advice — recall the flashed image of my passport at Æroflot™, and the sage counsel: *Run!*

In the twentieth century the Voice changed again when the radio speeches of Hitler led the populace down to Hell. That small shouting in the darkness was an early manifestation of the mechanically reproduced American Voice that now chirps and harps at us from every quarter to *Enjoy!*

Indeed, *Enjoy!* is what we *gaijin* TESOL instructors did best. Why not? We had vast CASH! reserves, so every weekend gathered to drink Kirin beer and play guitar. Kris now lived above a rice paddy, adjacent to a bust of Edison, in Otokoyama. Buddha may be the Light of Asia, but Edison made the bulbs — at first with filament made from Otokoyama's superlative bamboo.

Kris's fridge was packed with beer; sushi arrived by cartloads. I chatted with a fellow Canuck artist named Steve, just returned from Tibet. I'd thought the Land of Snows a fictional realm, from Tintin. Steve assured me it was real: real hard to reach, but worth the struggle. He planned a return trek, this time to the ruined temple of Rongbuk, sixteen thousand feet up Mount Everest — which the Tibetans called Chomolongma, "Mother Goddess of the World". The place was on no map, for none existed. Peking forbade their manufacture as a matter of national security. In short, Rongbuk was a ruined temple in a lost mountain kingdom: the temple in my dream! I'd forgotten all about it! Suddenly, though blotto, I was too thrilled to sleep.

With Erik and Josh I stepped over prostrate *gaijin* and crept downstairs, past Edison, past the rice paddy and into the forested hills, where slumbered an ancient temple. I climbed the wall and set off deafening alarms and blinding Kliegs. We fled along a mile-long corridor of shrines. My training had paid off, and when we reached the end and flung ourselves down a forested slope and hid beneath that town's famous bamboo I thought, my heart beating like *kodo* drums, I've never felt so fit! Now I can go to Tibet and find that dream temple!

But how? Even China lay out of bounds, except to groups chaperoned by government shills. And then there was the climb. I was no mountaineer. Yet nor was Maurice Wilson — a British explorer and eccentric I read of while finding out what little I could about the Land of Snows.

In 1933 Wilson set out to claim Everest for Britain. He had no training, or even sense, but he had a plan: fly his Sopwith Camel up to Rongbuk and climb to the peak fuelled by pure Will. By May he'd reached the North Col, where he vanished in the snow. A British expedition found his journal the following spring. As late as 1960, climbers sighted an unknown tent a thousand feet below the summit on the very route Wilson tried to climb. There was a ghostly chance he'd reached the summit first! Small wonder Britannia had ruled the waves! Today they could not even rule themselves! But I could! I was fit! Assisted only by Schrödinger's Cat, I could create my own reality, and conquer the tallest mountain in the world! That week the *Japan Times* ran this headline:

EVEREST MAY NOT BE
TALLEST MOUNTAIN

"Can you believe it?' I said to Guinevere. She looked up from the little calendar on her Player's™ cigarettes and said, "I missed my period!"

We bought an early pregnancy test, mixed fluids in a little vial and covered it with a blanket, for neither of us could bear to watch it slowly change colour — or not. I saw I'd inadvertently recreated Schrödinger's evil thought experiment. What of it! If my theories were correct this was the time to prove it, by choosing the world of adventure, and the temple in my dream.

But suddenly it seemed a lonely road ahead, straight on till mourning, with nary a curve or a surprising view. The Voice was clear on this: *Let go!*

So instead of thinking I felt and fumbled for Guinevere's hand, and together we pulled aside the veil.

CHAPTER XXXVII

THE FAMILY

*An unexpected party — A message from
my unconscious — Mr. Osaka (Runner
Up) — I witness hot monkey sex*

R OB, BLACK SHEEP OF THE FAMILY on Guinevere's side, arrived suddenly from Thailand to
find us celebrating good news: we'd inadvertently
founded our own small dynasty. Guinevere was over-
joyed on both accounts: she had not seen her brother
since he'd run afoul of David's central family planning.
The eldest, he was slated to become a doctor. But he
hated blood and loved to teach, and was skilled at it; so
sought a TESOL gig in Nippon, and might he stay with
us till he established a foothold?

I could not picture David in his Stalinist aspect. I
recalled him as the gentlest of men: Lao Tzu nursing
his stunted beans. But in business, Rob said, he had
been ruthless. *Ruth*-less. And could he use our downstairs bedroom till he found lodgings?

We told him he could have the whole house in a
month or two. We were bound for home. The joke
about a man born so ugly the doctor slapped his mother
was here no joke: when my friend Mitsu screamed in
labour the nurse slapped her, hard. "You're going to
be a mother!" she cried. "You must be strong!" For

this, the hospital charged ten thousand dollars. Neither Guinevere nor myself wished to be slapped that hard. We'd rather hie to Chestermans and raise the child in paradise. There was only one big dark cloud on the horizon: a minimum wage, strapped to the Wheel of Time.

But then a sort of miracle occurred: I woke up laughing! I scribbled a sketch and fell back to sleep.

MARY, JOSEPH, BABY JESUS AND THE MANAGER

At dawn I found I'd scrawled a crude nativity scene. I showed Guinevere; juice shot down her nose — a good sign, for (to paraphrase Nietzsche on science) the thing about humour is, either it works or it doesn't.

This work was drawing and writing both! It was the *subtle interplay* between image and text that gave the thing its juice-shooting power. I might make more than minimum wage by selling its like to newspapers. It sounds fantastical to we moderns, but in that golden age a living wage might be obtained from such.

Rob had meanwhile ensconced himself in the downstairs bedroom and begun to preen for his first interview. His chief defect was his looks: women lined up so he felt no need to settle down, but saw a lonely road ahead, though he had three daughters back in Kamloops, and might he borrow a shirt?

But due to weight training mine were all bespoke, for the neckholes must be fitted to my simian girth. My trainer, Hiro, beamed with pride whenever we ran laps. He was a lovely man, whose heart was bigger than my quads, and held the title Mr. Osaka (Runner-Up). On his desk sat a silver-framed photograph of him in competition, snatching and grabbing for the gold. This seemed a bold move for a Japanese; closer inspection revealed the photo was of Hiro's *sensai,* Mr. Osaka (First Place) — not a mere also-ran like himself.

On hearing my glad tidings he laughed with joy. "You will be a Papa!" To celebrate, he took us to Mino-o Shrine. He pulled up outside Number 666 Seiwadai Higashi in a red pimpmobile that filled both lanes of our thin street. He had not slept, so great was his anticipation of the Big Day. At last! I had a chance to *amæ* properly. I'd let him do the driving, and the paying, though I was flush with CASH! Hell, I'd let him diaper me if I must.

Mino-o shrine is famed for its deep-fried maple leaves and monkeys — to which species I am related, for when I was six my baby brother Mickey was such. His birth mother was killed on the road to Jinja; my mother weaned him with mashed bananas and milk in an eyedropper. His greatest joy was to sit at table with the family, solemnly laying down his spoon at grace. Now at Mino-o we watched the fun as a female thrust her engorged buttocks at a scrawny male, a simian *salaryman*. He was inside her momently, in front of my pregnant wife, there on the dappled path! Had he no shame, or guilt? No: it was subtler than that.

A massive male arrives, an Emperor type. "What's this? My concubine trysting with my slave?" The two uncouple and feign disinterest: each looks the other way. The Emperor turns his back; the couple trysts. He looks: they stop, and gaze in opposite directions. Convinced — not of her fidelity but of his hegemony — the Emperor struts away. All three are gifted by this cuckoldry: the Emperor with power, the female with a reserve protector for her babes, the *salaryman* with hot monkey sex, and the whole clan with genetic variance. To win these gifts, all they must do is look the other way at the right moment.

Hiro and Guinevere, Rob and myself laughed merrily, then drove home to Seiwadai in the big red pimpmobile.

CHAPTER XXXVIII.

OPPOSITION

I fail to amæ — Mickey the monkey —
The blind spot explained — The role of the
deviant — A new hope

EN ROUTE, A TERRIBLE OPPOSITION was born in me: my gym-honed belly demanded carbs, and soon! But I'd seen Hiro surreptitiuosly counting his last yen in quiet desperation. I could not indulge further on *amæ*; nor could I survive the journey home unfed. Surely my friend did not wish me dead? So I suggested we stop for Dutch sushi.

Words fail to paint poor Hiro, turned chump by his *gaijin* friend, slumped at the sushi bar, his Big Day ruined. He drove us home whey-faced and never spoke to me again. I tracked him to his office once, but only glimpsed his leg as he ran round a corner to escape. I was bewildered. I'd thought myself adept in Japanese ways, but was no more a member of that clan than Mickey had been of our human family.

That wretched creature's fate was sealed by butter — for if there was butter in the room, he thought of nothing else. At table he tried to restrain this butter-lust, but as we ate his fervor grew till finally he lunged at the dish and seized a leathery fistful of the golden stuff, and shrieked like steel on concrete when my father tossed him out the kitchen window into the garden, where he sat weeping in high dudgeon and eating hibiscus flowers.

He grew so wild he was sequestered in a cage on the veranda. One night the sky above the Rwenzoris flashed with thunder. Mickey went berserk, screaming and ratttling in the dark, while I hid under blankets, safe inside. At dawn my brother and I walked out in our pyjamas to find he'd strangled himself trying to squeeze his head through the cage bars.

Such opposition between lust and restraint described my gimbling situation. I sought to cast off my habit, to clear it up like a rash: to be a stretcher-bearer in times of war, on good terms with all. But now I wondered: was a there a warlike opposition built into the very structure of being human, as with the human eye?

The diagram on Page 5 of this book shows how the eye is designed, or rather has evolved, so that the optic nerves leave in a single bundle at the point midway between A and B. Where the nexus exits there can be no rods or cones: thus forms the *blind spot*. The Reader might easily locate his own by use of the patented diagram below, included here for schools at no extra cost:

To activate the diagram, hold the book at just the right remove — perhaps twelve inches — and close the left eye. Now move the noggin forward and back while focussing on the "L" and, *presto!* — the "R" is gone! Fallen into the blind spot entirely.

When both eyes are open this *lacuna* is filled with information from the opposing peeper; but *if thine eye be single*, errors arise we cannot even be aware of. And culture is nothing if not a singular vision of the world. This is why Outsiders like myself — artists, homosexuals, Libertarians — are essential to a culture's health. The question is not: Are freaks good or evil? but rather: How much opposition can our culture afford?

That summer the human family was confronted with this question directly, in the story of Mathias Rust. A German teen, despondent as Young Werther over the Cold War, Rust left his parents' Hamburg flat and set out to oppose the dominant paradigm: that East and West are born antagonists, and all of us but helpless pawns condemned to watch this grunch of giants from the front lines.

Like Wilson, Rust had no skills, or even sense. But he had a plan: he'd fly his rented Cessna over the Iron Curtain, land in Red Square, and thereby build an "imaginary bridge" 'twixt East and West!

He tore the back seats out of the Cessna's tail section and refitted it with auxiliary fuel tanks. He'd flown

R™

less than fifty hours, so practiced by flying to Iceland, and there visited the house where Reagan and Gorbachev had fallen out over Star Wars.

Bolstered by this success, he refueled in Helsinki,

then on May 28th turned his Cessna east, killed his instruments, and flew blind as Luke Skywalker along the Baltic coast into the most heavily-policed airspace on the planet.

MATHIAS RUST: OUTSIDER

CHAPTER XXXIX.

OBSTRUCTION

*A dolorous stroke of bluck — Bastille
Day — I step up my training regimen —
Weightlifting vs. yoga — Disaster! —
The Harmonic Convergence*

EN ROUTE, RUST FACED OBSTRUCTIONS terrible
and divers, armed only with beginner's luck, or
bluck. The Cessna was variously mistaken for an oil
slick, a flock of geese, a friendly aircraft and a rescue
helicopter, while a chicanery of bureaucratic incompetences allowed its tyro pilot to slip past four phalanxes
of Soviet air power.

May 28th is the national holiday of Russia's border
guards, and much of the Red Army was drunk that
day on the contraband vodka that flooded in to fill
demand created by Gorbachev's ban; for, free or in
chains, the market has its way. When Rust reached
Red Square it thronged with tipsy Muscovites; so he
alit on an adjacent bridge where, as *bluck* would have
it, city workers had that very morning dismantled the
overhead trolley cables and would raise them again
the following day.

Thanks to this string of long strange quarks Rust
penetrated the Iron Curtain as if it were no more than
a mirage; an idea; a mental barrier — and the Evil
Empire naught but a state of mind. In terms of cre-

ating his own reality *à la* Schrödinger, he'd shot that damned Cat into space.

I read this in the *Japan Times,* which was my sole source of news in those vagabond years, and distorted my view of them. I heard naught of Max Headroom or MC Hammer, yet the Harmonic Convergence commanded several entries. From these I adduced there was some syncopation of the stars that somehow aligned with the Mayan calendar, and if the human race joined hands at certain spots, including Mt. Fuji, instead of nuclear deluge there would be transformation, world peace, free daycare, and in short, the Earth would shine like the sun!

UNKNOWN ICON, 1987

But first things first: if Rust could ring down the Iron Curtain, then surely I might overcome the lesser obstructions between myself and Rongbuk.

The first obstruction was Guinevere's natural affection. She wished to cuddle and read books while she baked our little bun, and wished I might jaunt through China, find my stupid temple and hasten home to her in a month or less. I estimated no less than three.

On Bastille Day I took her to a famous restaurant in town. At table we learned the food was not famous, only the waiter. The walls were hung with photographs of him waiting on TV. Undaunted, I proposed we travel as far as Shanghai together, thereby decreasing our separation and increasing my temple time. I told Guinevere of the Peace Hotel, its *haute* and cold cuisine and gilded bathtubs. She scoffed! Shanghai was a filthy hole — the baby would get hepatitis and die! I said only if she *chose* that reality. She called me an animus-possessed flake and threw a glass of water in my face, and fled the restaurant weeping.

I knew I was a victim of her hormonal state, but I'd learned much in Japan about the nature of apology, and how a sincere one might grease the palm of Fate. I apologized to the famous waiter, ran after Guinevere and apologized to her, confessed I was indeed an animus-possessed flake (though at the time I knew not what it meant) and reduced my offer to six short weeks. When she saw how much it meant to me she acquiesced, lest I subconsciously blame the child.

The second obstruction was the climb ahead. The average elevation in Tibet is sixteen thousand feet; the air is thinner than a Welshman's smile. Even to blow one's nose requires superhuman effort. So I ratcheted up my training program, ran ten miles each night, and lifted weights the size of train wheels that bent the bar and made me feel like Superman, though not in the Nietzschean sense. Guinevere meanwhile traded her nicotine addiction for yoga classes and began stretching on the living room floor for hours. I scoffed! Yoga? It was but weight training for girls! She should try real exercise some time.

Guinevere said flexibility trumped brute strength; I said I stretched an hour before each session; she said such amateur elongation was not yoga, which also enlarged the soul, and I should try it if I ever felt strong enough to bend. We ended up on the carpet between our two pianos, which neither of us could play, hauling each other back and forth with our legs split wide and our feet soles wed, till I felt a massive *twang!* as though my spine were a doorstop, bent double and released.

Next day I could not get off the couch, which gave me time to reflect. I'd sought escape from the prison of my head by nurturing my body, but in truth my head had merely whipped my body into shape the way a drunk in Dickens might whip an orphan. How could I climb Everest from my couch? As I lay groaning Guinevere suggested acupuncture. She was now deep in her first trimester, with nary a bout of morning sickness. Why not see her man in Kyoto, Angus-*san*? I simultaneously saw acupuncture as *mumbo jumbo* and my only hope — we sailed for Shanghai in a month.

CHAPTER XL.

DELIVERANCE

Angus — Oor Wullie — The subtle body — Tibetan dæmons

NGUS, MY DELIVERANCE FROM PAIN, turned out to be no oriental sage but a burly Scot whose red beard and white smock made him look like a colour negative of Santa. He'd left Glasgow many moons ago, and had a Japanese wife and children, whom he supported with his acupuncture practice, a small clinic in the old quarter of Kyoto.

The rooms were dim and hung with charts and *sutras.* The furniture smelt of sandalwood and camphor. Angus examined my back and explained briefly how acupuncture works: existing simultaneously with my physical body, superposed upon it, was my *subtle* body. There was no physical reality to it, he stressed; but hale health required both bodies be attuned — "Ye know *whit* ah mean?"

But I was thinking that his spiky hair recalled a beloved cartoon character of my youth, Oor Wullie, who sat on an upturned bucket like a little Buddha and each week in the *Sunday Post* endured the typical reversals of Scottish working class life with stoic humor. Angus laughed. He loved that urchin too, and at once we were as friends.

He soon had his new friend splayed on a table, while he explained the structure of the subtle body. It comprised seven nexuses arranged along the spine, called *chakras*. Cosmic energy — *kundalini* — flowed into this system through the lowest of these, the root *chakra,* at the base of the spine. Thence it rose through all seven till it blossomed into the thousand-petaled crown *chakra* and flowed back into the cosmos. On its ascent it must be transformed into a higher frequency at each *chakra*. In this they played the part of gearwheels: "Ye-kno'whit'ah'*mean?*"

But I was picturing Oor Wullie on his bucket,

laughing while his seven chakras spun like cog-wheels. Angus claimed my injury had buggered my subtle body's powertrain so that I was stuck in first gear, and going nowhere, least of all Tibet, unless he could unblock my *kundalini* by jamming a dozen nine-inch needles into my spine.

At this point my mind grew marvellous clear, for though I do not number injections among my phobias, I hold *tabu* all subcutaneous needlework: tattoos, piercings, or the series of rabies shots I'd need should dogs bite me in Tibet, for they were rumoured to be rabid, and the temples were full of them because —

"Done!" said Angus, and clumped a Chinese herb called *moxy* on the needles' daggery ends, then lit the stuff, so that I resembled a Hawaiian *luau* and its *tiki* torches.

He said with mock chagrin, "You've been running on concrete! Ye might as weel tak' a ball-peen hammer tae yer spine. There's not a running shoe in this *wurrld* that'll protect ye from the impact! Unless — un-*less* ye get a pair o'thae new ones frae' NASA, they've got metal cups on the soles that flatten oot and pop *baack*, so ye'r actually — bouncin' — alang — on — springs!'" He kangaroo'd the table's length to demonstrate, head hung sideways in the manner of Charlie Brown, so he might meet my eye. I momently imagined leaping up and tearing the needles out, screaming. The telephone rang.

"Hullo!" he said. "Aye! Aye! Aye … Aye. — aye. AYE! Aye, aye, aye — look, ah cannae talk noo' — but did ye hear aboot the TV set in Los Angeles? During the Harmonic Convergence an angel appeared on it! They unplugged it, and hit it wi' a hammer — eighteen hours noo, an' the angel's still on it!   Well, Ah have tae go! " *Click!*

He waved his moxybustion stoor aside. "So you're goin' tae Tibet?   Ah just went tae a *slide* show aboot Tibet!" Coincidences were piling up.   "One o' the pictures was o' a statue that embodied *pure evil!*   They had tae cover it wi' a blanket just to take the picture!   They just lifted the corner a wee bit, so ye could see one o' its toes?   Well, that was enough for me!   The shivers went up an' doon ma' spine, an' a sez at the break tae ma' pal, 'Did ye see it?'   He sez, 'The Pure Evil?'   Ah sez, 'Aye!'   He sez, 'Och, Angus — it ga'e me the *wullies!*' "

"Not a month later, a man comes tae ma' door, an' *he's* been in Tibet, doin' high altitude research, wi' electrodes taped tae his nipples, ye'kno'whit'ah'mean?   So he's sittin' ootside a temple listenin' tae the monks dae their chants, an' suddenly he comes oot o' his boady an' goes shootin' up intae the sky!   When he sees his wee boady, so far away, he doesnae *like* it, he goes scrabblin' back doon intae it. But when he gets back inside — there's sumthin' else in there *with* him!   Ye'kno'whit'ah'mean?

"By the time he got tae ma' place, the left side o' his boady had *withered*.   He sez, 'Can ye help me?'   Ah sez, 'That depends.   How long'll ye be in Japan?'   He sez, 'Aboot a month.'

" 'A *month?*'   Angus made shooing motions.   " 'On yer way!   *On yer way!*' "   He leaned over until his face was in shadow and said, "Because between you an' me, it'll take aboot fifty gene*rations* tae get rid o' that thing!   Ye'kno'whit'ah'mean?"   Then he plucked *oot* the needles and made an appointment for the following week, which I kept, because his *mumbo-jumbo* worked.

CHAPTER XLI.

DECREASE

*Seiwadai & environs — Mie — A
game of go — Flowers of flame — The
motorcycle dæmon*

NOW DID I DECREASE the time spent lifting chunks of metal from A to B; which left space to explore the hills around Seiwadai, where the world slipped back centuries from tarmacadam to terraced tea plantations. In tall grass aged *obasans* hunted snakes with sticks and baskets, and at the forest wall farmers grew *shiitake* on stacks of rotting *shii* branches, as if Basho might momently trudge past, complaining of ulcers and penning the masterful *haiku* that Japanese children since the Eighteenth Century have been forced to memorize in practising calligraphy:

shizaukasa ya	the stillness
iwa ni shimu-iru	shrilling into rocks
semi no koe	the semi's cry

They say no *gaijin* grasps the deep context of Basho's words, and that may soon be true for all: by *semi* the World no longer meant an insect, but a kind of lorry.

One night my private student Mie arrived with a plate of cookies. She'd gone shopping for a dress, but when she saw herself in the changing room mirror she was dismayed by the effect. Instead of returning the dress to the rack she returned home with it, and wept. We laughed at this typically Japanese folly, drank iced coffee on the veranda, and listened to the whine of *semis* and the motorcyclist who nightly rode through the hills above Seiwadai at *shinkansen* speeds, perhaps a teen driven mad by Examination Hell. Such Outsiders, or *kichigai* — crazy spirits — are esteemed, for they play the part of safety valve for the group, who are accommodating to a fault. For example, my neighbour Obayashi came for tea with his children, and rather than cause a scene sat groaning with shame while his little girl stood on the couch and tossed pillows at the pianos till they *plinked!*

I walked Mie home; for though crime was unknown, strange things were done in the dark. Once, a man ran up behind Mie and punched her on the head. But now the night slipped past silent as a pickpocket. The only lights came from the little police booth and the doorway of the *go* club.

The room was stiff with smoke from a thousand

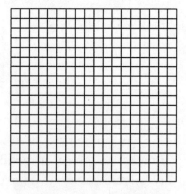

**WHITE TO PLAY AND WIN
IN A TRILLION^{TRILLION} MOVES**

Camels. Half of town's male population sat and fumed in rows, as once had reeked the factory chimneys of Glasgow and Manchester. When I requested instruction old men gaped as if they'd seen a talking horse. They adumbrated the rules, and I saw go was no Asian cousin of chess, but its mirror'd twin.

For chess begins with perfect order: black and white face each other in stasis, then the opposing armies clash over possession of the squares until the battlefield is empty and chaotic. Conversely, go begins with perfect chaos — the void of an empty board. It is played out not on the squares but on the lines between; and the opposing forces of black and white build up till one devours the other whole.

I told all this to Erik when he arrived that weekend with Jocelyn, who played piano while we drank and sang past midnight, then heard our neighbour screaming at us through the wall. Next evening the poor fellow lay slumped against the beer machine outside the bank clad in his underpants. His wife apologized. Work had been difficult of late: he'd clocked seventeen-hour shifts all month.

This so-called work ethic is yet another aspect of *amæ*, whose unanswerable demand to dissolve oneself completely into the field of dependent love is transposed into economics thus: the *salaryman* seeks *amæ* in return for services rendered; yet no amount of work will suffice unless it end in death. Hence the Japanese saying: *kono shigoto o kyo-ju ni shiagenai to domo ki ga sumnai* — "I won't be happy if I don't finish my work today."

Of course, a *salaryman's* work is never done, so to counterbalance the pain of being strapped always to the Wheel of Time they seek to vanish into a collective blur of alcohol and chanting. The end result is long hours, plus festivals at every turn.

Thus *Bon Odori* hit like a monsoon and the entire population repaired to their ancestral villages — even the dead, who hovered in the heavens till their descendants set ablaze huge *kanji* on mountain-tops to serve as landing beacons. Whole shires drank copiously, and though the archipelago was tinder-dry, bought fireworks — *hanabi*, or "flowers of flame" — set out in bushels at every toy shop. One Saturday Erik arrived with Kris, burner of shirts, to find me setting off a hundred dollars' worth.

We could not decipher the instructions, so each blossom came as a surprise. They burst like bombs, or shot like rockets, or spun like Catherine wheels. One did all three: swirled sparks across the tiles, shot skyward and detonated with a great retort that showered detritus on the rooftops all around. In the smoky silence silhouettes bobbed like fearful hand-puppets at lit windows. Dawn came; a thousand *salarymen* stood by their beds like giant toy soldiers ready for their wives to dress and dispatch. I met Obayashi on the street between our houses. He said:

> *very loud fireworks*
> *late last night*

and while I marvelled on deep context he rolled his Kawasaki into his garage, at which I realized this taciturn fellow was the motorcycle dæmon of the hills.

CHAPTER XLII.

INCREASE

*Heat — Wrestling Gaijin — I scale the
Great Wall — King Charles' Head — A
new world*

DEMON-LIKE, THE HEAT INCREASED till every
shirt was damp and every tie hung loose. My
school threw a bash on a rooftop in Umeda, where
spent TESOL instructors splayed on plastic chairs
beneath blazing *tiki* torches. I waltzed Guest House
alumni Brian around the roof while his brother Matt
laughed, then we three gazed down at the sex arcade
where once I'd tried to force *amæ* on Jack. "There's a
whole world of sin down there," said Brian, wistfully.
Matt meanwhile told how at night he raced his motorcycle through the hills behind his town at suicidal
speeds. "I feel compelled," he said. At the bar Midori
lowered her sooty lashes, her cotton bodice white as
snow cranes, laced tight in strategic regions, elsewhere
flowing into petticoats, as she listened to the goateed
kwatteiru from Mino-o. Good luck to him, I thought.
I'd bigger fish to fry.

For I'd begun to write and draw whole worlds. For
years I'd drawn but one thing: the Great Wall in my
head; first from the front, then from above, then from
every other angle. The drawings were brutal with

detail, yet void of subject — all context and no content — for I feared the only content would be gimbling scenarios.

THE GREAT WALL IN MY HEAD (UNFINISHED)

I also wrote continuously, yet only wrote one thing: a scientifiction tale about a cosmonaut who must cut off all his limbs to fit through a malfunctioning teleporter, and thus escape his ailing spacecraft. I had other ideas too, yet no matter what I set out to write I ended up rewriting that one tale, till Guinevere took to calling it King Charles' Head, after the Ouroboran

Mr. Dick — David Copperfield's lunatic uncle, whose ambition to complete his memoir is thwarted by the constant insinuation of King Charles' Head into the narrative arc.

But now, with Erik as sparring partner, I wrote for sheer fun a series of one-act plays, wherein we two appear as *Wrestling Gaijin*, and partake of Japan's high culture, such as the ancient tea ceremony, but always end up grappling in spangled tights, smashing through paper walls and *tatami* floors. For we had noted that no matter how we tried to master Japanese manners, still we were seen as all-star wrestlers who might at any moment try to impose each upon the other a *full body press*, a *forearm smash*, or even the dreadful *shining wizard*. Yet once we were resigned to our roles we both felt much relaxed — for paradoxically, taking on these caricatures resulted in a closeness with our true selves.

Inspired, I dashed off King Charles' Head in the hours I spent each day entrained from home to work; mailed it to an American scientifiction magazine, laughed angrily as I read the rejection slip to Erik; then set out to pen an epic fantasy graphic novel.

I couched the tale as an illustrated travelogue, of the sort popular in *fin de siecle* Britain: an account of a pilgrimage made by a polymath scholar named Fin, who sets out to debunk the divers mythologies of his world only to find that though they are not real, they are still true. When it was done I saw the opening chapters were vague, and so rewrote them. On finishing I found the whole less than perfect, so started on a third round, upon which Guinevere declaimed: "It's King Charles' Head again, just bigger!" I scoffed! There was no comparison between the two, for this new work was *illustrated*. Behold the frontispiece: Fin's study. Clearly my mind was much improved, for now the entire contents of that imagined world lay jumbled in the foreground, while the wainscoting of the Wall was sequestered to a top shelf:

FRONTISPIECE FOR AN UNFINISHED EPIC

CHAPTER XLIII.

SEPARATION

A slow boat to China — Korea — Nanking — Shanghai — The Bund — The Peace Hotel — A close shave — Mao

WE MUST NOW SEPARATE ourselves from the Land of Wa, so in September climbed the gangplank of a rusting Chinese freighter with a million yen sewn inside one of Guinevere's stockings and slung round my waist. Our *sayonaras* had ranged from official to poignant. Takahachi, over costly sushi, said: "We are different. But I respect your strange way of life." Tanaka feared I might jump from a window in Nepal while addled by hashish. I told him the word he sought was acid, like the milk. Parting with Erik was no great sorrow, for the man is a monster whose ego rivals that of Kim Il-Sung, the Emperor of the north half of Korea, which land we now skirted to the south, into the China Sea. As the last limbs of Japan's archipelago dropped astern I felt bereft. No more *oshibori* or *Wrestling Gaijin*.

Such moments of separation are critical in *amæ* theory. While other languages must use recent technical terms such as "separation anxiety disorder" to describe these crises, Japanese have for æons used the commonplace word *hitomishiri*, said of an infant who has begun to recognize the essential Otherness of his mother.

But while the vocabulary of *amæ* might smooth such rites of passage, it does not guarantee success. Japan's poor behaviour in World War II might even be seen as *amæ* run amok. We can no longer imagine the extent to which that country had by the Thirties succumbed to its own Little Emperor system. Consider the barroom scene in Ozu's *An Autumn Afternoon:* Sakamoto, the little sailor who'd served under Hirayama in the navy, asks why they lost the War. Hirayama shrugs and says it was probably for the best. Sakamoto nods. "At least the militarists can't push us around any more."

The rest is context; for the iron bands that bound their culture like *furo* rings had long since tightened into torturous device. In counterbalance, the nation felt compelled to export *amæ* to the lands around, as I had tried to force it upon Jack. The result: divers disasters, still felt today. Korea became a suzerainty run by a Japanese-trained team of propagandists, who after the War fled north and conspired with Kim to devise a sort of super-Matriarchy. For though the West sees Kim as the ultimate Patriarch, those early spin doctors portrayed him as a sort of *Ur*-mother, spreading blankets over exhausted students, while State-sponsored folk singers wailed of him:

> *I cry out forever in the voice of a child*
> *Mother! I can't live without Mother!*

In China the outcome of forced *amæ* was so terrible that stories of it were proscribed by Japanese law, and only rumours swirled around the Black Hole of Nanking, which region our ship now fast approached.

On the second day we crossed the tail of a monsoon. The sea was yellow with soil washed down the Yangtze, and furrowed like a field with massive rolling waves. The ship climbed each thirty-foot swell, balanced on the crest, then plunged into the trough while rivets cracked like ricocheting bullets. Guinevere succumbed to morning sickness, and lay in our little cabin, whence she claimed she astral-projected back to Japan.

On the third morning I spied a radio mast and a long low wall. By noon we plied a waterway clotted with craft of every size: rusting behemoths like those in vintage jigsaw puzzles; freighters like our own threading between these giants alongside sailing ships, dingies, yachts, and motor launches; and far below, black barges with forges flaming on their decks, ringed by clusters of skinny *sanpans* whereon families went about their lives like fleas upon an elephant, hanging laundry, frying eels in smoking woks and casting nets between the diesel slicks.

We berthed at the Bund, where stone towers built by money extorted from the populace during the Opium Wars jumbled along the banks as if chunks of Manhattan had fallen from the sky. The customs agent forced us to exchange three hundred thousand yen into scrip called Friendship Exchange Coupons. On the street I traded these for local bills called *yuan*, at twice the Friendship rate. The dock was piled with contraband Japanese televisions, over which men and women fought, punching and slapping each other hard, while in a nearby booth two policemen played cards, their blazers hung on hooks.

Shanghai's ten thousand taxi drivers worked on

quota; by noon they'd fulfilled their social contracts and now were parked under ten thousand bridges playing *mahjongg*. So we strolled along the Bund on cracked macadam through clouds of plastic and dust while filthy omnibuses belched monoxide stoor, with windows missing and thickets of brown arms hanging through the holes. Granite and marble edifices once grand as the Empire State were now festooned with laundry lines and ducks on poles and wicker baskets. People shouted and shoved and spat. After a year of smiles and bows I was delighted by this slackening of standards; Guinevere, less so. In the restaurant of the Peace Hotel she dispatched me to the kitchen, where I observed steam boil from giant kettles, condense on the filthy ceiling and drip back into the noodle pots. When I returned with this grim intelligence my wife had formed a plan: eat only hard-boiled eggs, drink only Coke™, and fly back to Japan at dawn. And so she did, leaving me to play *l'etranger* in this strange land.

CHAPTER XLIV.

ENCOUNTER

*Feng — Minimum wage in Shanghai — I
am filled with melancholy — Born to shop:
The gathering imperative*

I HAD A STRANGE ENCOUNTER the next day with
a native of Shanghai outside the strangest art store
I had ever seen — and I've seen many, for though I
own few clothes, no car and just one spoon, in places
that purvey the tools of art I am content to shop as was
my Grannie at Lewis's Department Store in Glasgow,
where my brother said of her, "Give her a canteen and
a shilling and she'll be happy for a week."

The strange art store was clearly once a cinema.
My sundries were place in a bag along with my CASH!
and zipped up to the old projection booth on a wire,
whence disembodied hands plucked it and retracted
like the tendrils of a sea anemone. For several minutes
I watched pairs of these hands swirl 'round the wares
sent up to them, lit by shafts of sun that streamed from
the opening, like ghosts from a forgotten film.

My purchase zipped back down along with change
in numerous tiny crumpled bills, each worth so little
there was no point in uncrumpling them. The cashiers
tossed these in expert handfuls on the counter, the way
my grandfather, a Glasgow baker, tossed handfuls of

flour and sugar into bowls and thereby always reached th'exact ratio, yet could not explain his craft in numbers. These tiny bills afforded glimpses of the hinterland — not in the untrue images of jolly proles, but in the patina of oil and grease from real factories, fine yellow dust from rice fields caught in folds, smudges of red ink from chops and seals, and tiny scaffolds of Chinese characters scribbled in teetering towers down the margins.

As I pored over these on a park bench near a statue of Marx and Engels, a thin young man in a threadbare shirt approached. I'd seen him in the art store, watching me shop. I nodded hullo; he asked in clear calm English if I was lost, or needed help.

I told him I must find a barbershop, a canteen and some climbing rope. He nodded. His name was Feng; he was an artist for the State. Just like those phantom taxi drivers, he worked on a quota for a minimum wage of thirty dollars a month, based on his age. Just like his parents, he painted watercolours of birds — presently for the ubiquitous telephone cards that everyone in the world now used to place long-distance calls. But his apartment faced south, and in the summer months became a glass furnace. Heat made the paper too absorbent: if he leaned on the parchment it wrinkled, and his work was ruined. So he filled his quota in wintertime and spent the summer walking in the Bund trying to stay cool. Despite the penury he obviously endured, the fate of this *flaneur* who followed the seasons seemed more humane than being strapped year-round to Time's Wheel.

We found a barbershop in the lobby of the Peace Hotel, beneath a filthy wall-painting of a tiger that must have once been grand. A shave with strop and soap and straight razor calmed me, for after baring my throat to a random denizen of this new land I knew there was no nationwide conspiracy to murder me.

Canteen and rope, Feng said, might be purchased at the People's Friendship Store — but that place made a mockery of its name, unless one holds friendship to be empty, expensive, and full of government shills, who smilingly redirected us to outlets where we might find what we sought. We walked for miles and came upon a loading bay along a crumbled alley, where six old men in simmets played cards, drank tea, smoked and spat.

They told us there was no more rope: the factory now made only plastic bailing twine, of which they had a surplus. We reached the canteen outlet to find it gone. The factory had modernized, and now made only ceramic pump-action carafes with orchids painted on the front, perfectly unsuited for the Plateau.

The afternoon sizzled slowly as we described a great circle 'round the inner city. Its rubble and smoke recalled the ruined metropolis in *Dhalgren*, whose buildings burn yet never collapse, caught forever in the amber light of Fall. I found myself filled with a vast nostalgia for the Glasgow of my childhood, turned by Hitler into rows of rotten teeth; for Edo's wooden Tokyo, consumed by Yankee flowers of flame; for Rome, put to the torch by Goths; and for ruin itself, the red light that shines at the end of all these blinded alleys, and felt that yearning mediævals called *acedia*, and deemed the root of sadness.

By late afternoon we had walked miles with nothing to show but friendship. At last Feng suggested the People's Number One Department Store, a relic from Shanghai's Roaring Thirties, whose wooden escalators were the first in Asia, and whose sports department might stock rope and canteens.

MARX IN THE AGE OF MECHANICAL REPRODUCTION

CHAPTER XLV.

THE MASSES

Marx and Spencer — A new Nativity —
The Ghost Train — Chengdu

T HAT MARX CALLED RELIGION the Opiate of the
Masses tells us he never saw the masses shopping.
Perhaps he sent his maid. The People's Number One
had seven floors of shopping, and all were fabulously
dim from lack of electric light. The cavernous ceilings
were smudged with lamp soot, the elevator shafts dark
empty pits. Ragged shoppers swirled up and down
the stairs like souls from Dante in their Mao no-size-
fits-well pyjamas. At every entrance shifty sorts sold
synthesizers whose cheap syncopations clashed midair
with Red Chinese opera blaring from speakers that
could never be shut off. The entire stock was on display in battered pyramids: tins of food, hand-cranked
adding machines from the Fifties and cutlery fit for
camping with refugees.

Feng and myself swirled up to the sports department
on the fifth floor, where the attendant sternly informed
us that the People had no time to waste in such vain
pursuits as mountain climbing.

Chastened and returned onto the street, we passed
the impressive corner window, its glass curved like a

Hopper painting. Gold light spilled through it onto the pavement, where rows of blue-smocked proles stared reverently through the glass at Sony™ products — Walkmans™, televisions, tape decks — nestled in straw like a technological nativity. Beer costs a dime, I thought; these must go for a song. But when Feng made inquiries, none of it was for sale. The display was but an advertisement. Feeling they'd failed to grasp the concept, I said, "But if you can't buy the stuff, what's the advertisement for?"

Feng thought a while and said, "The Future."

We dined at a restaurant near the train station, which featured tiny rocks in rice, plastic tablecloths, and velvet paintings of the unclimbed mountains. Feng reacted to the bill as one might to a wedgie; but post-Hiro, I was too gun-shy to assist.

The station was an endless cavern of tracks and platforms. Hidden among them, Feng found the fabled "ghost train" — a gift from East Germany to Mao whose berths were unaffordable for people like Feng, so rattled across the land empty as the *Mary Celeste*. I threw my gear down in a Pullman car with lace curtains, brocaded upholstery and scrimshaw of castles on the Rhine. The bunk had linen sheets. But the greatest luxury was a volume control on the speaker that blared rhetoric and cacophonous song from dawn till dusk.

My friend was awed by the decadence I would enjoy: the tiny halfmoon sink hid under the table, the oiled wood, and most of all, the scrimshaw, which he scanned eagerly for detail before the guards shunted him away, so quickly he was barely able to slip me his card. Then the train trundled past Nanking into the marginal lands that lay west.

At dawn, through the swaying window, I saw mountain gorges hemmed with narrow roads where harvest grains were laid on the macadam so passing cyclists might thresh them with their wheels, in the odd belief that "every little bit helps". I saw dwellings so shoddy the setting sun shone through their seams; and an old man rocking on a chair amid such static poverty as only central planning might sustain.

Lest I bring down the government I was locked in to

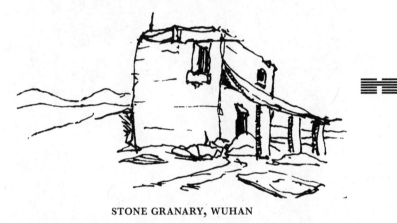

STONE GRANARY, WUHAN

my fine quarters — save at meal times, when a woman almost bent under her massive army hat unlocked my door and led me past a row of empty compartments to the buffet car, its lace tablecloths and red carpet sheathed in plastic. On the third day I found out why: a shift in the landscape, and suddenly I had company at lunch who dislodged fish bones from behind their teeth onto the table, then cleared their throats and spat upon the carpet.

On my return I found the corridor full of passengers. Chungdu lay close ahead, now made an economic experimental zone by the twice-purged Deng Xiaoping, who promulgated freedom of the market. The effect was instantaneous: a thousand businesses bloomed, including that of seven window dressers my age who showed me photographs of their work in their compartment; and when I reached my own I found therein an aged derelict in a stained simmet leafing through my sketchbook, smoking.

SOLDIERS AT A STATION, SICHUAN

CHAPTER XLVI.

PUSHING UPWARD

*The Engineer — The Academic — The
Hump — The Forbidden City*

HIS TEETH WERE GONE, his face was crumpled as the currency — yet he was a master engineer, constructing a great dam somewhere inland. He had destroyed whole regions, but it must be done. He placed his worn clawed feet up on the seat across the aisle as if to bar my egress and said almost with pride, "China is very old. Very poor."

We talked till Chengdu then rode by rickshaw to a concrete inn grim as Hitler's bunker yclept, like much in China, the People's Number One. At dawn I set out on foot towards Tibet, but on the road met travellers returning thence who cursed and said they'd hitched westwards three weeks only to find the border sealed tight as a Welshman's purse.

Dismayed, I returned to the Number One and in the lobby saw a bearded fellow haranguing the hoteliers for smoking. He had one leg hoist on a stool, wore an outback hat and spoke fluent Mandarin. His name was Bruce; he held the Chair of Asiatic Studies at Melbourne University, and also a life-long fascination with Tibet. Although it was forbidden he planned to fly from

Chengdu up to Lhasa — for as a "foreign expert" he carried papers granting him the right to purchase local plane tickets. We talked, and drank, and next morning he purchased two.

The ærodrome was blue with cigarette stoor. NO SMOKING signs hung everywhere; none noticed. Against this fog Bruce raged, a fresh air Canute. At the critical moment our ticket agent struck a match: Bruce, tense as a junkyard dog, swung his cane at a sign right by the fellow's head and screamed in Chinese. The man, as if waking from a dream, was not rankled by this foreigner's policy but stubbed his smoke and barely glanced up as he wrote our chits.

The plane propellers hummed a note that rattled teeth and windows. The snacks hid nutshell; the illustrations of disaster on the safety pamphlets were terrifying. We flew straight up the face of a mountain range called the Hump, which until recently no Chinese plane could climb; and in the icy waste pilots still sighted an unknown fang of rock some forty thousand feet in height. The Chinese had kept all intelligence of it hid.

I told Bruce I was soon to be a father. He said, "Prepare to feel left out." My babble of Japan as matriarchy he deemed unsound; then over Burma nodded off and woke with a cry. He'd dreamed of a return to his childhood home in Adelaide. A shadow stood atop the darkened stairs. "Mum?" he asked, timorously. A dreadful voice boomed: "NO!"

"Oh God, it was awful!" he said, eating my stony snack. As he chewed the plane descended over miles of derelict Red Army trucks and helicopters, a dusty monument to the folly of any great nation that invades an ancient desert land to save it from itself; then we alit upon the Roof of the World.

The door cracked open, air hissed out, and kept on hissing out, until I felt I'd landed on the moon without a helmet. The Plateau's air holds half the oxygen of sea-level stuff. He who scales its ramparts slowly doubles his quota of red blood cells and is safe. But he who simply pops out of a plane like a stripper leaping from a cake runs the risk of inflaming his brain tissue, whence it may puff up like toasted wheat snacks causing painful death. It was a chance I had to take.

Lhasa is built on a flood plane 'round the varicose river that bears its name. That afternoon Bruce and myself tarried by that river, watching women with photographs of the Dalai Lama stuck in their hat- bands wash thick quilts with their feet, stamping the cloth into the silty sparkling water and laughing at the strange spectacle of us.

The light was dazzling; the atmosphere gave so little shield that sunburn and frostbite might strike simulta-neously. My sunscreen bottle had puffed up like a cod jigged too quickly from the deep. I cracked the seal; trapped air hissed out. Ink from my pens had simi-larly bled from the nibs so that all my gear was black and sticky; and this selfsame process was unfolding in my skull. The sky, a deeper indigo than I had seen outside a cinema, pulsed and seemed to race at me. Bruce, in singsong voice, began to reminisce about his childhood then trailed off with a faint "Oh my! Oh dear . . ."

We walked to the heart of that dusty reeking town: the Jokhang Temple, which Bruce called the "holiest of holies". I argued that, once holy, surely it was all the same. Near this holy or ultra-holy place we found lodgings at the Snowlands, whose rooms were spartan, with painted wooden beds, thick dusty quilts and bare stone floors, empty but for three young Frenchmen: Damien, Marc and Marc.

In the dust-caked lobby I found a copy of *Tibet Transformed* by one Israel Epstein, a Maoist who'd clung so tightly to his beliefs he'd strangled them, and whose official account of Tibet was so at odds with all

I'd read it seemed impossible to reconcile the two. So I let let them lay alongside each other in my head, like quarreling lovers.

CHAPTER XLVII.

OPPRESSION

Drawing vs. Shutterbugging — Drepung — Oceans of Wisdom

Tibet's oppression was deemed by some to be irrelevant until the cameras arrived — though I had none, for photography seemed to me a sort of fetish that stood between the traveler and the place. Many I met in Tibet were not *there*, but had returned home, and in their minds already showed slides to friends of places they'd never really been, and of locals who so feared the camera they must be paid to pose.

Conversely, drawing anchors a man in time and space. When I look long enough to draw a thing I fall into my *wyrd* the result of its geography; for the place is like unto an armed fortress, ringed by ramparts built up fifty million years ago when India collided with Asia, rumpling the earth's crust like a Basset hound's hide. So great is the elevation that one might glimpse the planets at midday! And he who holds the high ground has the advantage — thus the surrounding empires of India, China and Russia have sparred over it since they were made. Yet of those three, China alone lays a legitimate claim.

For in 1275 Kubla Khan appointed Tibet's first

and melt mysteriously into it. As I sat staring at various crumbling doorways in the old quarter of the city its denizens would emerge like flowers after rain; approach and silently observe; then bring yak butter tea. On my third day I cycled to Drepung Lamasery and sat outside the gates to priest-king, Phagpa; and in 1337 the Chinese helped repulse invasion by India's Muhammed Tughlag. In 1653 the Fifth Dalai Lama swore allegiance to the first Qing Emperor, who sent an army of craftsmen to construct the Potala. Its iconic curved roofs spring from the Chinese wont of providing nooks for airborn drag-

GATES OF DREPUNG LAMASERY

draw. Two nomads in a tent watched for a while, then brought out a bat- ons to curl up and roost. Therein, the Dalai Lama ruled for centuries, and

tered boombox. Through crackles came the pop of Sam Fox singing *"Touch me! Touch me!"* She was become ubiquitous.

Within, I drew a street view while a tall monk watched and beamed.

when his body failed, reincarnated himself. In 1933 when the Thirteenth died, monks at Lhamo Latso saw in the Oracle Lake a house in China where he'd been reborn. His predecessors Eight through Twelve all met

INSIDE DREPUNG

We drank tea, then climbed a mile of steps to the School of Philosophy, where I watched an exam. The highest mark went to he who won the

untimely ends (mostly by poison) before they reached majority; so for a century a series of Regents managed the land to the benefit of the ruling Dagsha Clan. Yet

loudest laugh. It seemed more akin to stand-up than religion. The grassy courtyard's walls were burst by mortars, through which I glimpsed below the vast ruin that was once the largest lamasery in the world, till it was razed by Mao Tse-tung.

Fourteen returned to that same house where he'd been murdered five times!

The Dagshas and their peers owned all Tibet — not just the property, but the souls. The Fourteenth was repulsed by this, and in 1954 discussed the matter with Mao Zedong.

Returned to the Snowlands, I sat to draw the courtyard's antique well; but my *wyrd* was shattered by a large American set on drawing water, who knew not how to "prime the pump".

He called the Chairman the "timely rain", returning with the slogan: "Socialism In Tibet Now!" For Mao was resolved to free Tibet and its People, whom he saw as the great Well from which he drew his strength.

CHAPTER XLVIII

THE WELL

*A large American — The pilgrim —
The French contingency — Steve — Yak
burgers*

HE HAD NO DOUBT if he only flailed hard enough, so worked the handle like *nunchuks* till the pump's metal throat screeched and rasped. I begged him to pour a little water in the top; he glowered at me, for none enjoys public censure save its instigator. But my pleasure was clouded by a sense that I was causing just as much damage to this ancient place, yet could not quite see how.

Kudrys, the hotel maid, saw my Canadian passport and asked, "Do you know Steve?"

that the well would flow for him, as the People of Tibet were in great need, enslaved by superstitions that infected every mind, from the serfs on the Plateau to the Living God in the Potala.

A peasant who saw a hat blow down a road attributed its motion to evil spirits; and even the great Lamasery at Drepung was afflicted by such magical thinking. For it was held that a monk who did not learn his *sutras* would reincarnate in a lower form — an insect, plant, or even (God forbid!) a Welshman.

But if he came back

WOMEN ON ROOFTOP, LHASA

I smiled and said Canada was vast, with many Steves; then on the high street walked right into Steve from Kris's party in Otokoyama! At a tea house we drank millet beer, or *chang*, while he rolled hashish into spliffs the size of clown shoes — for here, *ganja* was called local tobacco, "which the grinning rustics love to smoke".

Next day Steve struck out across the Plateau on foot while I luncheoned as a dog, frequented his old stomping grounds, and heard the *sutras* he'd ignored in life chanted aloud, he might still advance. Thus strays were never shooed away, and the grand temples were overrun by rabid mutts. To end this mad thralldom to unreason, Mao proposed he and the Dagsha Clan build a "Freedom Highway" from Chengdu up to Lhasa, connecting their two great lands and thereby increasing trade. In 1949 it was com-

REAR VIEW OF THE POTALA PALACE

with Damien and *les Marcs* on yak burgers and bread fried in yak grease — an *entree* stolid yet delicious, so I ate two, then lay athwart the wooden bench and groaned, reflecting on a Scottish schoolboy jest whereby we memorized the map of the Near East: *If Russia attacked Turkey from behind, would Greece help?*

Indeed it did: it plugs the pores, forestalling dehydration. The next day I was recovered, while both Marcs were felled by the altitude, and nursed abed their bleeding gallic noses while Damien and

plete; in 1950 the Red Army marched up it and liberated the Land of Snows. In 1959 the Dagshas and the rest of the elite fled by mule and yak across the Himalaya into Nepal, along with all the gold and treasure they could carry.

Once freed, myriad first-hand accounts of atrocities emerged from peasants who had been forced to hold targets in their hands for rifle practice by the ruling class; from boys who'd narrowly escaped the tradition of being buried alive under towers so that their souls might hold up those structures for eternity; from sci-

myself strode next door to the Holiest of Holies.

Outside we saw a one-eyed pilgrim who had walked untold miles to the Jokhang, prostrating himself all the way, and now trembled on the threshold of his God.

Conversely, I had come by plane, so felt a touch unholy. Damien entered that sacred place while I stayed on the steps and drew a row of monks from Drepung who sat cross-legged in the square.

entists who found religious relics made from maidens' bones; and farmers who, on trumped-up charges, had their eyes gouged out, their hamstrings sawn and their Achilles tendons snipped with pincers — a real-life Crab Thing horror.

The nexus of these attractions was Drepung, whose abbots imported and sold opium, lent CASH! at usurious rates, and when their debtors fell behind in payment took them into lifelong bondage.

CHAPTER XLIX.

REVOLUTION

*Thesis, antithesis, clusterf__k — I draw
at gunpoint — A big "thumbs up"*

EVERY REVOLUTION comes as a shock to the elite. In Lhasa, They were Us. When an earthquake shook us all awake Bruce said, "No worries!" For these, like fortune cookies, came by the bagful and were filled with portents all ignored. When monks saw a rainbow in the Oracle Lake we scoffed. Meanwhile the Dalai Lama addressed the United Nations on his homeland's woes. China's official stance was the one trumpeted in *Tibet Transformed,* which makes no mention of the million who starved in the Seventies.

In 1959 the monks at Drepung took up arms and fought to maintain their brutal status quo. They failed. Thanks to Mao's Great Leap Forward, literacy increased sixfold, and the populace learned to smash the Five "Olds": Old Customs, Old Culture, Old Habits, Old Ideas. (What was the fifth? Oh *damn*!)

Yet this success was met with condemnation from the West, whose God is dead (and we killed Him!) yet holds in esteem the Buddha, whose disciples propped up the Dalai Lama's murderous regime.

That morning I thought none of these things: I merely drew. When I was done a monk standing at the temple doors beckoned me in. Thus welcomed, I at last entered the Jokhang. The monk led me not into the sanctum, but up a flight of weary steps onto the roof, showed me a great gold *stupa* — symbol of the spread of Buddhism throughout the world — and bade me draw.

STUPA ON JOKHANG ROOF AT 9 AM, OCTOBER 23, 1987

Clamor rose from the square below; but I was fallen deep into my *wyrd* and paid no heed till Damien arrived to say the monks in the square were chanting. He ran to the rampart and looked down, and I was set to follow when a Voice whispered: *Schrödinger's Cat!* Perhaps this was the Revolution, perhaps a festival: I did not wish to choose, so sat and drew.

The hubbub grew till even Schrödinger would affirm the Revolution was upon us — and as with Sainsbury's™ strip-search, I wished to side with the oppressed. I picture myself astride the temple battlements waving a bespoke banner —

FREE TIBET!
WITH MINIMUM
TEN DOLLAR PURCHASE

then I picture monks snipping my Achilles tendons, so I stay still, and draw. The roof's aswarm with adventure types waving Canons™ and shooting everything in sight. Now comes a troop of soldiers waving guns, ripping film from those cameras. One runs up to me, but when he sees I'm drawing he stops. He's skinny as a stick puppet in his baggy uniform, and seems confused. His gun looks ancient: the bolt blacking has worn off from years of use. He shakes the barrel as if expecting coins to roll out. I point at the *stupa,* then at my drawing. He looks — nods — sticks up his thumb — runs away — Below, unseen army trucks screech into the square and worried voices caw through bullhorns. What of it? I'm drawing. A great shout rings the empty sky. Who cares? I'm drawing. The soldier returns — I show him the drawing — thumbs up — he runs away — as if I am surrounded by an invisible field of force — or fallen into a blind spot in the action —

the unseen crowd roars like distant surf — the world turns like Ken's order wheel — men chase each other 'round the rim: soldiers, monks, Chinese, Tibetans, locals, tourists — the selfsame characters, changing hats! I'm at the centre of this wheel, with no desire to choose a side. Some subtle power floods up my spine, and when it hits my heart I feel such pride that I have not succumbed to this charade it shatters the moment like glass, and down I come — down, down — then the soldier returns with two others and gestures at me, telling them to deal with this fellow and his protective bubble. But it was already gone. I'd sided with myself, and lost.

They hastened Damien and me downstairs into the sanctum at gunpoint. These things are never as one imagines in advance: for me, the Holiest of Holies was a small bare room, with army types sitting at a desk. Now I would pay the price of spiritual shenanigans. But wait — the soldier merely bade me show these higher-ups my drawing, whereupon thumbs shot up all around, hatted heads nodded, and then I was ejected with Damien into the square.

CHAPTER L

NEW WORLD ORDER

Lhasa under curfew — The Yak Hotel —
Tom, Hank, & two Jills — Mr. Chan

MAO'S MEN SET UP A NEW ORDER in the Forbidden City that night. The ancient doors of
Lhasa were kicked in one by one, and persons of interest
carted off to gaol. The rebel monks languished in an
army compound outside town. By dawn rumour held
the Plateau would be cleansed of Outsiders, save for the
Chinese.

Foreign devils scattered. Bruce used his papers to
procure a bus ticket and disappeared onto it amidst a
sea of cigarette smoke and hats. The last I saw of him
was his cane. A cartel led by an Australian named
Roger rented a bus and drove off towards the holy
mountain, Kailash, source of the sacred rivers Gan-
ges, Brahmaputra and Indus. The French contingent
had come equipped with a giant inflatable submarine
sandwich, and planned to photograph a monk biting
it, framed by the Potala, for a family friend who owned
a French fast food franchise and had helped finance
their trek. They now abandoned that plan and fled by
yak onto the Plateau in search of a village they'd heard
of but no western eye had ever seen.

I tacked a note up at the Yak Hotel, where adventurers traded climbing gear, socks and information. Next day a pair of ragamuffins bound for Rongbuk tracked me to the Snowlands. Both wore prayer flags as scarves, had peeling noses, scruffy beards, and wives named Jill, but otherwise were opposites.

DOORWAY WITH LIVESTOCK, NEAR THE YAK HOTEL

Tom was Australian and a doctor, as was his Jill. Hank sold display cabinets in Deroit, and must have hawked a goodly number, for he was outfitted in finest red Gore-Tex™, and schlepped a video camera big as a Basset hound. He was a friendly sort, but slightly tense. His greatest joy was telling others, with a rueful grin, "You missed it!" — be this sky burial, sunrise, or the last yak butter tea. He shouted at the concierge of the Yak Hotel, and cursed God when he dropped a lens upon the sand. But what of that? He was American — therefore I "cut him slack". Agreed, that nation stationed an apocalyps'orth of atomic ordnance in the Holy Loch next to my childhood home in Scotland, so that I woke in frequent *thunderplump* convinced the Judgement was at hand; and now Reagan, drunk on freedom, drove the world into the Future at such terrifying speeds the rest of us cowered under the back seat — but America was also home to my *Wrestling Gaijin* partner Erik.

From Chinese bureaucrats ensconced at the deserted People's Number One Guest House near the river, whose tiled rooms housed oxygen bottles for its putative patrons, we rented a Toyota Land Cruiser™ for a paltry sum. This was intended for jaunts around Lhasa, not one-way expeditions across the Plateau, but at the Lhasa Taxi Company Tom found Mr. Chan, whose father had followed Chiang Kai-Shek into deep disfavour, and who in the family's second generation of exile drove Han bureaucrats around Lhasa and worried that earthquakes might engulf him and his kin.

Mr. Chan agreed to drive us all to Rongbuk. Then, while I conquered Everest, he would speed Tom, Hank and the Jills to the Kodari Pass that led down to Nepal and return the Land Cruiser™ to Lhasa, where the Chairman would be none the wiser.

We paid him a month's wages for each day he'd spend outside the capital, and agreed that should the river in Rongbuk Valley rise above his knee the Cruiser™ would turn back, in which case I would proceed on foot. Outfitted thus, we passed the army checkpoint at dawn. An hour later it was in flames.

Unaware, we drove the "Friendship Highway" — which Mao proposed to King Mahendra of Nepal, that they might connect their two great lands, etc. — and

RUINED FORT, GYANTSE

arrived thus at Gyantse, an historic spot where in 1904 the British militarist Younghusband attacked from India and shelled the fort, yet respectfully left the adjacent temple intact. Then in 1974 locals roiled by Mao's Great Leap broke down the temple walls and freed the peasantry from the lamasery. The end result was ruin all around, amidst which Tom and Jill now luncheoned at a teahouse while Hank and Jill, outfitted with various multimedia components, stomped templeward in search of Holy Shit.

CHAPTER LI.

SHOCK AND AWE

I learn to count in Tibetan — Trouble with Hank — I play the part of Wizard — Chomolongma

A S FOR MYSELF, THE SHOCK AND AWE I'd witnessed at the Jokhang would suffice. Instead of more temples I increased my respiration with a trek, and on the plain behind the *chorten* met a band of pilgrims in robes ornate as tapestries, their yak-greased hair set with turquoise nuggets, beaten silver rings and copper bracelets jangling on their sun-cracked skin. Atop each brow the Dalai Lama rode in photographic form. When they saw my drawings of the Potala they gasped as one, produced a Frodo-style chalice set with *lapis lazuli*, filled it with *chang* from a grimy plastic petrol canister, and taught me how to count in Tibetan by plying me with quaffs at each mistake.

I did not reach the number five; an hour later I lay on my back, gripping the Plateau lest I slide off into space. Recalling my companions, I bade farewell and raced across the tops of ruins, skirting the massive temple wall until I saw the Land Cruiser™ in the valley below.

But now I was impeded by a pack of former monks who barked their shaggy *sutras* at me. I do not hold with hurting animals, among whose number I count myself; and the only cure for rabies involved an abdominal syringe the size of a billiard cue. Reasoning thus, I hurled a rock at their chief; it bounced off the flank of that wild creature, which curled its tail and lunged like Mickey for the butter.

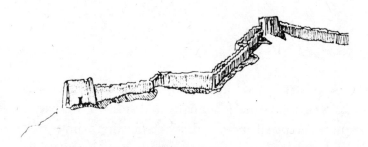

I ran in terror along the wall till I came to a gap wide as a grave is long, with those potentially rabid curs snapping at my heels. I flung myself through space; survived; shouted foolishly at the dogs; and stumbled down the bouldery slope to the Cruiser™. Hank glared at me, then at his watch: "That's the second time we've had to wait."

A day's drive west we ran out of petrol in a town beyond Shigatse that was a single windswept street, and seemed the last outpost of the human world. Then Steve shouted at me from a tea house door, his face burnt like a gasket 'round his eyes. He and Guest House Happy *alumna* Brigid, an Irishwoman of mettle, had hitchhiked here on pilgrim trucks and farm machinery.

We compared drawings and drank yak butter tea; then I performed a magic trick with the change. A cry of shock! A gasp of awe! I tried another. Soon half the town ringed 'round. Hank whispered gleefully, "They think you're a wizard! We gotta get this on camera!"

Seduced by my own glamour I watched him corral three peasants against the pocked stone wall, train his

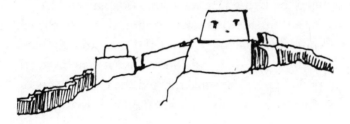

RUINED TEMPLE WALL, GYANTSE

instrument on them and cry, "Now! Go! Do it!" I pulled the old "chopped thumb" trick: they did not see, or even look, but glanced askance at Hank's enormous third eye till he unshouldered it. "Typical!" he said. "You turn on a camera, and nothing happens."

Was it irony? Satire? I'd lost track. Undaunted, Hank sectioned a sun-blasted peasant with a baby tied to her back. I chopped my thumb: she screamed and fled. Hank glanced around for more victims — but luckily Mr. Chan returned with the Chinese official irresponsible for fuel, who seemed surly and afraid, as though our cheerful chauffeur had shaken his lapels till petrol came out. The Cruiser™ was replenished; Steve and Brigid walked away into a field of winter barley; and suddenly I sensed I stood to one side of the Big Picture.

On the fourth day we made the river at the mouth of Rongbuk Valley. Mr. Chan dipped his foot into the rushing water — down, down it went, up to his thigh. "Oy! Oy!" he cried, and shook his head.

We reassured him that our covenant was firm — he need proceed no further. But he was keen to see Chomolongma, so drove until he found a shallow spot. In plunged the Cruiser™; water massed against the door and swept us sideways downstream, then tire clawed rock and the machine clambered onto the far bank like a drenched dog and shook until its engine died. He pulled apart the starter, dried the components on a sunny rock, and in an hour the beast roared once again.

We had outrun the road, so climbed a grassy bouldered field in spurts and starts up to the Pang la Pass, and as we crossed its saddle there rose before us the massive flanks of Chomolongma.

RUINED FORTRESS NEAR TINGRI

CHAPTER LII.

THE MOUNTAIN

*Wrongbuk — An unexpected meeting — A
terrorist act*

N O ISOLATED PEAK, THE MOUNTAIN was but the largest fang on a broken granite jaw that lay across the entire region. We stood at seventeen thousand feet staring at a sheer rock face, where the earth's crust had dislodged like a paving stone three miles thick. Below this Rongbuk Valley shone emerald green, split by the river's shining snake.

Three hours later we heaved and sputtered into the temple compound. Whither that wondrous sense of wholeness? All whispered "broken". The shrine was crammed with charred *sutras*, shattered Buddhas and yellow oxygen bottles that had been to the summit of Chomolongma.

At supper too many of us cooked a broth. Hank put a brave face on it, asking if Tom's Jill was set on becoming a doctor, for she might as easily become a chef. "It's a done deal," she said drily; for he seemed resistant to the idea she was already accredited.

I boiled tea, and a young monk with a sinus infection thrust his hand into the pot and grinned. His trick perplexed me — not because he had endured the heat, for our African home stood at four thousand feet, and my mother had to make tea in a pressure cooker lest the water boil at uncivilized low temperatures — but because I did not know where that stained hand had been, and so must make the tea again.

The mercury dipped ten degrees below the mark. I fell asleep listening to the monks chant *sutras* through the wall, then rose at dawn — no feat when mountains block the sun till noon — and strode along the river-bank a mile towards the mountain. I passed a smashed stone tower whose contents spilled out like seed from a granary: pressed clay tablets depicting dead Tibetan kings. Above that stretched a scree slope where every boulder had been carved with flowing Tibetan script: *om padme mani hum*. Mao's task seemed hopeless. How does a man dethrone God when He is etched into the very landscape?

Beyond lay a vast talus field scattered with thirty tents bright as confetti — all expeditions headed to the peak. A lonely wooden signpost said to none:

NO TRESPASSING
$10,000 FINE

Addend it it my bill, I thought, and gave the sign wide berth, as though this might reduce the fee. Around a twisting esker I came upon the base camp of the British Everest Expedition — deserted, save for the cook, who was from Glasgow. The mountaineers were climbing on the North Col but would soon be home for tea. "Climb high, sleep low," the cook said, and made the tea in a pressure cooker.

We sat gazing down the valley as the tent flaps rat-tled like prayer flags and the sun beat on our backs like Buddha with a golden stick. The tea was strong and sweet. The cook told me foul weather lay ahead — and also that a Japanese climber had died that day, not from a fall, but drowned in the raging river. Dismayed by this, and bolstered by the tea, I climbed into a gully above the base camp, and there I hit a Wall. I struggled like a swimmer underwater, then the wind increased till I could barely stand. I'd reached around eighteen thousand feet. A mile above lay the "death zone" where Chomolongma thrusts into the jet stream and no human can acclimatize, but only perish. "Climb high, sleep low," I thought.

Tomorrow I'd bid farewell to my companions and return, then try to reach the fabled "ice causeway" two thousand feet overhead. At the limit of my strength I took out a drawing I'd done down in Chengdu of Mao's giant statue, and set to burning it. The Chinese blame Japan for creating the Black Hole of Nanking, but Mao's complicit too, for it was a Nationalist stronghold; so he ignored the situation, to his benefit. Thus the tale went untold in either Tokyo or Peking.

Mao's concern was that the People progress along Marxist lines. Marx held the Western masses had gone from tribal communalism to feudal serfdom, then with the Industrial Revolution to proletariat, alienated from their means of production on the farm. Only then was the populace primed for Revolution. But China had no proles, only serfs; so Mao conspired to vault over the Enlightenment as if the game were leapfrog and create a proletariat from scratch, by industrializing food production with his Great Leapfrog Forward. When the People thereby landed in an abyss of central planning, instead of changing tack

Mao doubled down, till fifty million starved — a million in Tibet — from bureaucratic bungling. In memory of these myriads I now burned Mao in effigy.

But oxygen here was scarce as soap in Wales, and the paper would not catch. I huddled between two house-sized boulders and cowled my lighter till a pale blue blur inched down the drawing's edge; it caught; then in a flash the Chairman was gone.

MAO (REDACTED)

When I reached the plain below the base camp I saw that Tom, Hank and both Jills had ridden on the Italian expedition's supply truck up the route I'd fought so hard to climb. Hank and Jill carried the giant camera slung between them like a child in a hammock. Watching them struggle, I felt a rush of affection. They certainly were in this together. I must cut Hank more slack.

When I reached the temple my mind felt just like toast: I might spread jam on it, but should not press too hard. A ragged Frenchman in a dinner jacket and cheap patent leather shoes told me Lhasa was in flames! But we were safe up here; so I retired to my freezing cell and rested for tomorrow's climb.

CHAPTER LIII.

AUSPICIOUS OUTLOOK

I learn Tibetan by subconscious method —
Time stops — The Tao — Niels Bohr —
I meet with Yama, God of Death

T HAT CELL HAD NO AUSPICIOUS OUTLOOK: its
slatted window opened on a stone roof dotted
with black holes of latrines, and China's outlook was
less auspicious still; for the Population Bomb threatened a chaos worse than Mao's Great Leap. The
wind howled Mary, Joseph, Baby Jesus; the mercury
swooned and sank, and I drifted into darkness listening to monks chanting, chanting, chanting, chanting.
chanting . . .

I woke abruptly, chanting in Tibetan — which
tongue I knew not. Apart from that, the cell was silent
as a *ninja* mime. Mr. Chang's face was still as any
death mask. My lips grew numb, and I began to pant.
As Hayashi might say, "Mountain sickness: no joke!"
The brain, in search of oxygen, expands against the
skull and bruises itself to death. But first come halluci-
nations, and in this phase I slowly understood that Mr.
Chan was dead. I hovered over his corpse until I heard
a sort of squeak. He's still alive, I thought, and lay back
down, but now became convinced it was myself who'd
died: beyond the pale, trapped like an insect in the

dark amber of this moment, with its bleak stone walls
and heatless yak dung stove, and Mr. Chan's waxen
face turned up towards eternal night like a stale loaf.
Time's silent sister kissed my fevered brow till I began
to sweat with horror at the Tao: all actions, no matter how well intended, in Time lead round into their
opposite. Mao's roots reach down to hell, but his

YOU CHING, I CHING

branches hold up the starry welkin. He was the People's Number One Mass Murderer, yet simultaneously
saved them with his one-child policy, which delayed
the Population Bomb's explosion by half a billion.

They say no foreign devil grasps the deep context
of the Tao; but surely the Danish physcist Niels Bohr,
whose complex inner landscape contained natural
oppositions, made Toaist inroads with his Principle

of Complementarity, by which he hoped to resolve the paradox of light. "The opposite of every great idea is another great idea," he said; and when he was knighted, set the Tao symbol in the centre of his coat of arms. Visitors were surprised to see a lucky horse-shoe hung above his door. Was he superstitious? No, he said — but he'd been told the horseshoe brought

luck whether he believed in it or not. Einstein objected, holding as canon that "God does not play dice!" Yet experiment proved He not only played, He lost half of the time. Chance was more than just a key ingredient of the world: it was the secret spice that made the whole thing work.

Meanwhile, unknown my me, the parasite *Giardia* wended through my own inner landscape and now demanded an exit visa and passage back to the latrines whence it came. At that rude facility wind blasted down from icy peaks, and a ghastly grunt issued from the black hole between my boots. I loped back to my cell and tried to rouse the yak dung stove. What could account for such a noise? *Yeti?* Then on the splintered door comes a long, dull scratch, as of a single claw drawn down its lower half — too low for any human form. My heart fills with terror absolute as scientific law — then I yank the door wide and see a great dark

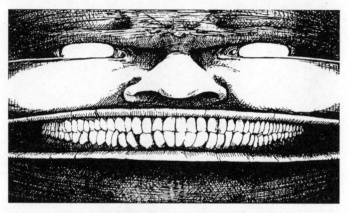

YAMA, ~~DOG~~ GOD OF ~~HEAT~~ DEATH

shadow crouched upon the doorsill that ambles past me and leaps up on my bed, bold as you please. A temple dog, big as a yak, black as Johnny Cash, and reeking of the tourist effluence on which it subsisted in the depths of the latrine. Despite the awful stench I thrust my feet under its warm flanks and felt glad of the creature's company. At last I dropped down into sleep, like a coin into a well, and woke to find the world made new with snow.

CHAPTER LIV.

THE VIRGIN BRIDE

A new approach — Yet another unexpected meeting — To Katmandu by bustop — A Glorious Vision of Eternity

R ONGBUK, WHITE AS A VIRGIN BRIDE, rang with the laughter of monks throwing snowballs at each other. Just as the Scottish cook foretold, climbing season was done: now came the descent. My soul was glad; my plan was crushed. But I had a Plan B — hie to the sunny south side of the mountain, where weeks of fair weather remained, and try again.

We trundled down into the valley and bathed in the corruscating rapids. At Pang-la Pass we stopped again, and saw two figures climbing up the far side. As they grew from gnats into humans I saw with some amazement they were Steve and Brigid!

I clasped them to me, babbling clichés about the Roof of the World while they gasped for air and tried to glimpse around me their first view of Chomolongma, won by weeks of trekking. Their faces lit with joy; they panted like Lamaze instructors as they gazed on that tremendous scene, where humans were reduced in scale till all our griefs seemed small. Recouped, they stumbled into that vast wonder, and I was hard-pressed not to follow — for their magic seemed stronger than my own, which had been *chauffeured*. Hank said, "You're in the shot!" I turned to see him rehearsing yet another pan. It was time to impose upon him the *Shining Wizard* — but as my mind slithered on blood, a jigsaw moment: Hank was to me as I was to Steve. *Ouch!* I thought, then: *Arigato, sensai!* and climbed into the Cruiser™.

Two days later we plunged into Kodari Pass. All

TWEEDLES

around us rock gave way to grass, then bushes, trees and jungle. We pinballed corkscrews as the sky grew dark, skidded and stopped at a sudden line of trucks. King Mahendra's wisdom in building the Friendship Highway was now clear: he simply had not kept up his end. There was some trade but no invasion, for the road had been swept into the valley by monsoons, which every season carved more miles loose and flung them down the slope.

We bade farewell to Mr. Chan and gave him our excess Friendship Coupons. His face shone with delight and fear, for it came to three months' wages — yet he'd never spend it if mountains crushed him while he slept, which tragic scene he adumbrated in his wordless way, pointing at the peaks, then smacking his temple with a scream.

So he drove north, and we trod south, down into no-man's land through landslides strewn with boulders big as garden sheds, festooned with creepers and rho-dodendron, and came upon a strange hotel built into the very slope. Its toilets opened on a great stone pipe that channeled a river down the mountainside, onto which shone ovals of light from other toilets far below. We slept on plywood, and learned the extent of Lhasa's turmoil: the border was closed, the city forbidden once more.

The black market was here so advanced they came to us in our room, and traded rupees for yuan at rates so favourable my CASH! doubled again. Next day we pressed south on lengths of road hemmed in by land-slides. Busses sat marooned, while others had rolled like turtles down the grade, and in their coped polychro-matic husks the drivers now raised families and sold sundries to the passing trade.

The roadhead to Katmandu was clogged with bus-ses stuck in the mud around a bridge knocked sideways by a recent deluge. Hank and Jill sped away in an air-conditioned limousine while Tom, Jill and myself climbed on the roof of a local bus, which heaved its tin flanks down the mountainside and at every village paused to let more people on. How did they fit? The bus conductor's single lock of hair was set with a copper ring. Thin as an eel, he slithered out a window and up the side, rode like a surfer across his clientele, slapping them, shouting, grabbing rupee notes, then disappeared over the low rail into the carriage.

We three lay stunned on bolts of cloth, stoned on the oxygen, enmeshed with baskets, chicken coops and fez'd Nepalis, swaying through a jungle drunk with monkeys, past shops built of red brick and painted with advertisements for cocoa and inner tubes that uncannily recalled post-War England, as if these two great cultures had swung round in a waltz and each left traces on the other's sleeve. At dusk Jill's face lit up with awe. Tom gripped my toe and pointed. I turned, and — *!*

Framed by the dark green crowns of mango trees the Himalaya rose above the ruddy dusk like a race of ice giants. Their chiseled faces caught the light, the snow turned pink, the rock a shade of blue stolen from the sky; bases obliterated by haze, they seemed to float above the earth like giant moons. The sun descended, pink turned gold, melted and caught fire; then all resolved into dusky red, then embered darkness, flanked by centurion stars.

"You missed it!" Hank grinned wryly when we reached Kathmandu. (He meant the last room at the best hotel.) Already Jill was dressed in Nepalese garb; they'd showered and eaten fresh fruit. By tacit agreement we broke our fellowship then, bade our friends *adieu,* and found lodgings at the shabby Lhasa Hotel near Durbar Square.

CHAPTER LV.

ABUNDANCE

*Kathmandu — I encounter the Goddess
Ganja — Farewell to the Australians —
The Permit Raj — To Annapurna!*

ABUNDANCE IS A POLITE WORD for what awaited
us in Kathmandu. While crossing the plateau
we had subsisted on *tsampa*, a gruel of winter barley
slathered with rancid yak butter; but here the inns sold
pizza, steak, granola, German beer and chocolate *lattes*
— all in the same bowl, if one so desired. In Lhasa,
books had been so rare they formed a currency, which
I once used to purchase sunscreen and a hat; but here,
every second shop sold scientifiction paperbacks, Tin-
tin™ comics, books by Jung and Borges and Joseph
Campbell, and back issues of the *Whole Earth Cata-
log*, as if David's library wall had spread out from the
dream house into the streets and built a Town of Wonders. In one I found a copy of *Dhalgren*. This time, I'd
finish it!

Adjacent to the hotel stood a walled garden that
fairly reeked of roses. Hand-lettered signs implored:

COME DINE IN THE BEAUTIFUL GARDEN

"With the beautiful flies?" said Jill. "Not bloody
likely!" Behind the fly garden stretched a dusty alley

where I bought a chunk of hashish small and redolent as a tangerine. In my room I packed my new and ornate silver hookah and drew deeply from it. Save for Steve's "local tobacco", I had not indulged since Tofino, and was unprepared for what happened next.

I lay across my whirling bed awhile and listened to the sweet cacophony that drifted through the window. My room must look out on the fly garden, for I could hear water splash from a tap, a bicycle creak, children laugh and women talk. I lay there picturing this Eden till I thought: "Why not look upon it directly?" I went to the window — but found it was in fact a glass-doored cupboard. I had hallucinated the beautiful garden. I lay down again and tried to read, but was distracted by sounds from that phantom paradise. I rose, and rapped the cupboard's back to see if it was false — for I could distinguish every detail of my hallucination: a man laughs; birds cry; a lorry rumbles past.

Perplexed, I crossed back to the bed and saw the tapestry behind the headboard move, as though wafted by a draught. *Wafted by a draught.* I pushed the tapestry aside — but found it was in fact a curtain, below whose window lay the walled garden in my head, now real, its slate roofs silhouetted by carmine sky, more verdant and vesp'ral than I had ever dreamed. I lay down on the bed and laughed, till clamour from the unreal garden disgruntled me again. For I'd forgotten the mystery was solved, and wondered anxiously how could I conjure the sounds in such detail — unless I had gone mad!

I rose, and shut the cupboard door to block out the imaginary noise, turned to the bed, saw the tapestry, pushed it aside, recalled the garden was real, and sank down in relief; forgot again; began to fret on the hallucinated sounds; repeated every step; ricochetted between the bed, the cupboard and the window — bed, cupboard, window, bed, cupboard, window — till a knock came on my door. It was the police! Disguised as Tom and Jill! I wished I'd taken a smaller puff, or bought more of that sweet taffy. What if I ran out? We sat on the roof and drank rum while Tom read Ray Bradbury to us, performing all the accents: " 'I see you never!' " he wailed in *faux* Mexican; and so it was, for two days later my friends flew back to Oz, leaving me to attempt the sunny side of Chomolongma, solo.

It was the heyday of the "Permit Raj". To stamp my trekking permit for the Everest region took six hours, for the clerks assigned to paperwork a mystic power that made of the simplest tasks an ordeal that would test the patience of Gandhi. I made three rounds of the same office building. On my fourth I befriended a soldier, who clacked his rifle bolt sternly when the next desk jockey tried to "shine me on".

I stored my magic waistcoat, long pants and etcetera with the manager at the Lhasa Hotel and set out for Everest with only the clothes I wore, plus books and hashish — but could not find the bus! All day and next ticket agents tried to explain where the bus was located using elaborate pantomimes that confused me more than modern dance. At last I saw a bus with ANNA-PURNA daubed on its saggy brow. *One mountain's much like another,* I thought, and climbed aboard. That evening at Pokara's police checkpoint I pulled out my trekking pass for the Everest Region.

Damn!

CHAPTER LVI.

THE WANDERER

I violate yet another Asian boundary — Africa-or-India — The scourge of Progressivism

I WANDERED THROUGH TH'ADJACENT King Kong jungle until I'd skirted the checkpoint, imagining a day when I might cross any sort of border in Asia legally; for I'd entered Japan through subterfuge, China through paperwork error, Tibet through luck, and Nepal through no-man's land.

The route to Annapurna so teemed with tourists it was dubbed the Coca-Cola™ Trail. But as the buddhist monk Seung Sahn once said, when asked the most propitious mantra: "It is *Om mani padme hum* — or you could say Coca-Cola™. No difference."

Powered by this wisdom I puffed up beveraged slopes and o'er suspension bridges like a freckled steam train, reading hefty scientifiction pulps and slim volumes of English poetry. Nepal was so beautiful I could not render it in pen and ink; in any case, the selfsame dæmon that in Tibet had anchored me to every doorway now turned my eye inward, aided by hashish, so that I penned instead divers gimbling scenarios and tenebrous mindscapes so fecund they threatened to engulf my coracled brain.

My heart, conversely, soared — for I was at last repatriated to the jungle setting of my childhood, living among the animals. I'd never warmed to the way we moderns must play one-man-band in the symphony of life; nor had I ever recouped at finding myself wrung down from Africa's jungle branches onto the macadam outside Annette Street School in Glasgow,

"CRIKEY! I'VE JUST ABOUT HAD IT WITH MAN AND HIS CYMBALS."

a stranger in a strange land, shuddering with ague in my stiff camelhair *coat* and throwing up on my *shoes* — those patent leather shackles that pinched my small wild feet — where the only creatures for miles were humans and houseflies.

Nepal was just the opposite. Consequently, shit lay everywhere, in every colour, shape and size: great buffalo turds stacked against walls for use as fuel; sacred cow pies; dark currents of sheep droppings; slick duck shite on door sills; pig dung stamped into soil. The variety so overwhelmed that under Machapuhari a skinny German girl taught me a euphemism — *lala* — and with her I wandered lonely as a cloud that floats o'er *lala* now and then, when all at once I saw a crowd, a host of *la la lalala*.

la la la la la la la la	(lying on couch)
la la la la la la la la	(empty, pensive)
la la la la la la la la	(flash, eye, third)
la la la la la la la la	(bliss, alone)

And then my soul with lala fills
And dances with policemen.

That this part of Africa — or India — is glossed in tourist literature is part of a larger plan: for the Future is bent on cleaning up the Past, regardless of consequence. My father's mission in Uganda was to build infrastructure, wipe out malaria and seed the youth with democratic urges. This noble plan soon went, as the poet wrote, *agley*: Obote, once democratically elected, set to plundering Congolese gold with the help of his Number One, Amin. That gentle giant was chosen for the task in part because he could lift ingots of the yellow stuff by hand; and was apprehended with several in a suitcase at the border; then when Obote went abroad Amin seized power, declaring himself Lord of All the Beasts and King of Scotland, and the *lala* hit the fan.

CHAPTER LVII.

THE GENTLE

*Lala land — The Myth of Modernity —
The Population Bomb — Two kings, two
queens*

OR THE GENTLE GIANT now had a dream — not a metaphorical one, like King's, but an actual nocturnal vision — wherein all Outsiders were purged from the Plateau and Uganda was free at last! As King, his dream was law. Foreign devils scattered. My father had already fled, dispatching our little family back to Glasgow while he stayed on to fulfill his contract, then striking south into the heart of that bright continent by train and horseback. *En route* he stopped to visit the King, William Wilberforce Nadiope, the Kyabazinga of Basoga.

The palace was deserted save for an old gardener trying to corral hundreds of baby chicks that zigzagged on the royal lawn. "Help me!" he cried.

As they worked the old gardener told of his dream to become a chicken farmer. He'd purchased a thousand chicks from a British company, along with feed and hutches. None came. He placed the order again: still nothing. A third attempt brought *nada;* then that morning all three shipments had arrived at once. The result was chaos: it took the men an hour to contain the yellow devils. When they were done my father asked if he might see the King. The old gardener said, "I am the King."

Amin deposed him, then buried half a million of his own clan's ancient enemies in pits. Such is the effect of Progress upon Africa-or-India, yet still we hold that benefit accrues naturally from Industry. It is sacred to us as a Hindu cow, even when the numbers do not jibe. Consider the Population Bomb:

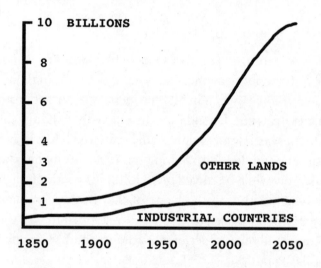

Clearly the selfsame freedom that led to the invention of our machines also birthed its twin: self-restraint. But in Africa-or-India our methods give birth to paradox.

I'd heretofore found paradox suspect, a kind of trick or ruse; but after seeing it put to use in Japan, took to it like a thirsty man to beer. And there was such variety! Asia's divers cultures were veritable microbreweries of paradox. What is the sound of one hand clapping? For me, it is the noise my mother made while commanding me to "be here *now!*" But in Japan such *koans* are tools, used to dethrone Reason and destroy the barrier between the observer and the world. In China, monks use *zen's* grandfather *ch'en* to align themselves with the eternal round of *yin* and *yang*, wherein all things paradoxically transform into their opposites. And India — the source of *zen, ch'en, et al.* — floats in an ocean of paradox, for they hold both parts of reality's puzzle in constant superposition. Even gender was here conflated. In one hilltop village I came upon a little *hijra* — a boy with female genitalia. Rather than trouble with toilets and pronouns, such magic creatures are deemed touched by God, though many end up as sex trade workers, because for a pimp, any excuse will do to party.

As I progressed, all supposition foundered 'round me. In my childhood tales the sun was male and the moon female. Japan inverts this with Sun Goddess Amaterasu and her brother moon, Tsukuyomi; but India has it both ways, with stories of twin celestial couples: male and female suns and moons. The plot involves a hunting accident: the male moon dies, then the female sun dies from grief. Thus enters death into the world, and is welcomed as a boon, for it ends all suffering.

The tale recalled my astrophysics professor, June, who lived with her physicist husband Ted; a cosmologist named Max; and his wife Millie. I held their cabin to be rustic till I saw their home: a rambling farmhouse where their two daughters, one from each union, ran up and down the stairs while June played "Barbara Allen" on the upright. I once watched all four take a day to hammer a single nail upon which they planned to hang a hurricane lamp. They went about their task in such a way that all seemed impermanent; for theoretically the nail might be pulled out and returned to the bag, then driven back to the hardware store. Perhaps they'd over-thought the situation; but they worked in deep space — their smallest unit was a billion. It was a wonder they could hold a hammer!

The same might be said of India, which sprung up round the Indus River ten millennia ago when the rest of us dwelt in holes and huddled from the night. Along the Indus they invented almost everything — money, cities, God — and while we fumbled with small digits, already thought in trillions. But their greatest triumph was the creation of the number *zero*, upon which pivot consciousness revolves.

CHAPTER LVIII

JOY

*A vast conspiracy — The Number of the
Goddess — The double slit revisited —
Everett*

EVEN INDIA'S STORIED JOY OF SEX leads 'round
that circular number to the pain of death. This
natural cycle is written into their cosmic law thus: At
the Creation the all-seeing Eye of Brahma opens, and
the cosmos blossoms for 432 billion years — a Day of
Brahma. At the zenith a tear forms: the water washes
away the world in Deluge as the Eye closes; then come
432 billion years of darkness — a Night of Brahma.
Together these comprise a Twenty-Four-Hour Shift of
Brahma: 864 billion years — one *Dwarpa Yuga.*

Joseph Campbell (who unbeknownst to me lay
dying the same day I set out upon the Coca-Cola™
Trail) tracked this mysterious number from India to
Iceland, unearthing it from holy texts where it lay hid.
In each, the number describes a cycle of Creation and
Deluge. In the *Epic of Gilgamesh* it is the cumulative
lifespan of the Ten Great Kings who reigned between
Creation and the Flood, when the Gods destroyed
humanity for disturbing their sleep with constant fes-
tivals. In the Bible it's the number of weeks between
Genesis and the Flood (again rung down by partying)

encoded in the alotted lifespans of the Patriarchs, from Adam to Noah. Even far-flung Iceland's *Edas* tell of 800 warriors who walk abreast through each of Valhalla's 540 massive doors, and thence to Ragnarok, wherein the world sinks beneath the waves. Do the math: that's 432,000 Norskies.

Clearly this is no coincidence. Many monks spilt much ink to make it thus. The reason for this vast conspiracy is clear: such wisdom — that all returns to dust — threatens the *status quo,* which to hold power must lay claim to eternal truths, when they are merely promulgating local customs such as individual freedom, expensive justice and the hot pursuit of happiness.

The West sees itself as exceptional to such; yet we are part of this great tradition, thanks to the double slit experiment that caused me such discomfiture on Chestermans. Recall: we know from Young's 1801 experiment that light cut in half by shining it through a double slit forms interference patterns, like a wave:

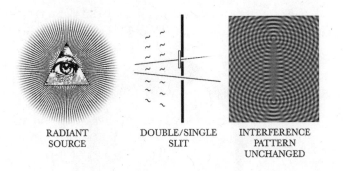

RADIANT
SOURCE   DOUBLE/SINGLE   INTERFERENCE
                      SLIT   PATTERN
                                        UNCHANGED

We also know from Einstein's 1905 experiment that light comprises particles that *ping!* What if we combined the two, by shooting individual particles of light through those double slits, one by one? Reason demands that since an individual particle cannot interefere with itself, the interference pattern will disappear. The experimental evidence begs to differ.

This nonsensical result led Niels Bohr, in 1927, to propose his Principal of Complementarity: at its deepest level, reality cannot be cut in half. Schrodinger, in 1935, showed mathematically that if one tried to do so, the world itself would split in two, and thenceforth both would exist simultaneously. In 1956 Hugh Everett III, a Princeton student, proved this occurred with every subatomic event: each particle at every moment forked both ways at once, each leading to a different branch of reality. He called this unimaginably vast jungle of forking paths the Multiverse.

Scots have a word for this: *mumbo-jumbo,* which Mungo Park brought back to Glasgow from Africa. But the thing about this *mumbo-jumbo* is, it works. Thus science bequeaths the thorniest of problems, for if everything occurs, then nothing matters. The equations function, but their effect upon the individual soul, free will *et al.,* is utter annhilation. Thereby the Western soul returns at last to the snake-infested Eden that is India.

HUGH EVERETT III, MASTER OF THE MULTIVERSE

CHAPTER LIX.

DISSIPATION

The Deluge — The Eye of Brahma —
Whiteout!

EVERETT FELL INTO DISSIPATION: he ate, drank and smoked himself to death at fifty-one and had his ashes thrown out with the trash. I knew exactly how he felt. Along the Coca-Cola™ Trail I smoked so much hashish I might as well install a chimney, and was beset by snacks and beverages at every turn, of such low cost I soon stopped counting. In Tofino I had scrimped for months to set out on my travels, but now had lost track of my money's worth, and felt like that British character dubbed the *fox*, who leads the steeplechase through town by throwing fistfuls of coloured paper upon the sod. Yet no matter what pittance I paid for food and shelter some large Australian boomed: "Ya spent *how* much? *Thirty-seven cents!* You were *had!*"

Embedded with this crew, I seldom met a local. At sunset we stomped into villages and shot the natives; at dawn we took Poon Hill, famed for its roundhouse views of Annapurna V, or III — I'd long lost track. The air was rent with whirring shutter blades as the entire phalanx faced East and CLICKED! to arrest the sunrise. It was a kind of hell we'd built with tourist CASH! where for a sawbuck grown men must carry our stuff uphill all day, and be glad of their employ. I thought of Paul (who'd furnished my first intelligence of Japan) when he returned from Europe. "How was it?" I inquired; he shook his head and handed me a card that said:

ACROPOLIS NOW!

I'd seen this play before, in Tofino, where we held Outsiders in such contempt that when a German stepped back to shoot his family and was swept off the rocks at Cox Point, instead of mourning we laughed

("Ach! Papa ist kaput!") and said he'd paid the fair market price for dislocation from his environs. Now I knew exactly how that German felt. Around me, all that was solid went up in puffs of hashish smoke. *Holy shit,* I thought. *I've never been so high;* except perhaps the time I ate two hits of purple dragon acid and spent the afternoon barfing up what seemed to be the single eyeball from the back of the Yankee dollar. Perhaps this was the True Path, and I should just keep going. *Fade into the jungle with Captain Kirk.* Kurtz? *Damn! The jungle's lovely, dark and deep. But I have promises to keep. Perhaps a pipeful ere I sleep. Where am I?*

I looked down at the trail to find it gone. I'd reached a wilderness reserve between Annapurna and Machupahari, high in a jungle valley, in rain more torrential than Scotland's and heavier than Japan's. The only place I'd seen such rain was in Tofino. I backtracked till I found the trail — or was it a small creek? The trail forked; I bore left, downhill, an easier climb. But it led me to a cliff above a pounding cataract. I backtracked and found the trail again — but now it seemed to lead in all directions. I could not choose a route; and the twinned hemispheres of my brain were complicit, for Reason led me uphill to more forks while Emotion led me down to the cataract's ceaseless roar.

The rain turned suddenly to sleet, which in that jungle setting seemed as wrong as snow on citrus, or Austrian economics, yet it was real, and I was soaked, in shorts. I would not last the night. I wished I'd come in thick fast pants! I meandered in a mazy motion, then ran in panic, then sat on a stump and sobbed. I did not know it, but I was very ill with dysentery and would soon discharge a gallon of blood from nether regions. My mind had failed; my body was in revolt.

Thus wrestled I with me, and would have locked my head under my arm had I been flexible enough, as Guinevere no doubt was. *Ah, Guinevere! I see you never!* The child will grow up fatherless, like Theseus, Jason, *et al.* Hey ... wait a minute ...

Suddenly I saw me from without: red-faced, panting, drenched, my poncho swinging like a *jabot* round my neck. I trip backwards, roll downhill, clutching at roots and creepers, try to climb directly up the cliff — *I'm going to die* — the deluge has stirred myriad leeches to life, and these now crawl between my grasping fingers, up my wrists and ankles and down my neck, battening on every vein; and now, as my jumpmaster Bruce might say, comes the big white light ...

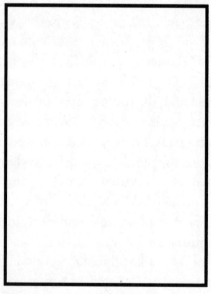

ME (REDACTED)

CHAPTER LX.

CIRCLE LIMIT

*I lose my religion — Leeches — A Little
Man — The hut — Other families —
The Covenant — Father*

L IMITED BY THE CIRCLE of my breath, I fall somehow into my *wyrd* and when the miasma clears
I'm cowled beneath a tumble of overhanging roots,
from which rain drips hypnotically. A final shaft of
sunlight slants under the clouds through the canopy
and catches on something bright a furlong down the
ravine. I make my way to it: a single stalk of wheat.
An ear. Ears of bread. *Pano mimi.* Agriculture. Civilization.

But why is wheat out here in the jungle? I see
another stem nearby and thresh towards it; thence,
as if recapitulating the emergence of my species from
African jungle to the first cities of the Indus, I glimpse
a low stone wall — a terrace reclaimed by jungle that
recalls abandoned situations in the parklands outside
Tofino; family homesteads reduced to oblong clearings
where rhododendrons still bloom. This wilderness
reserve must have been expropriated from farmers,
like the airport at Narita.

I run along the dyke for half a mile until the forest wall breaks, and in the last light see smoke rising

from the chimney of a hut. Outside stands a boy of ten, startled by this white man staggering from the jungle. "Lost," I say.

He tells in hand-shaped sentences how the storm washed away a bridge some miles below and trapped many tourists at his uncle's inn. His father has gone to help; he is in charge. He leads me to a barn; I peel my shirt off, and he recoils! Leeches suck on my every vein: throat, wrists, ankles, scrotum. I burn them off one by one with my lighter. They sizzle and burst until the barn reeks of frying blood, as pungent as a Welsh picnic. Then I follow the boy's lantern as it swings along the dark path to the hut.

Inside is tiny, hot, and full of shadow. An iron wood stove roars. In a recess reminiscent of my Grannie's bed of nightmares lies the boy's sister, fourteen, smiling blissfully as she suckles her newborn, a skinny, wizened creature, more ancient than infant, with a knot of thread pierced through one ear to show it is a boy. The girl rubs buffalo fat on him from a beaten copper bowl. He gurgles, fusses, and suckles more. *I'm going to live.*

Hours pass, and no one says a word. The boy roasts potatoes in the dirt beneath the stove, and we sit with our backs against the bed and our feet almost in the flames. I might nod off and wake to find them gone, as did Pinocchio. Gazing up, I see branches through the roof, and realize I only dreamed this refuge, and in reality lie dying amid the forking paths and thunder. The storm twerks nakedly against the door, the baby coos, potatoes hiss, and the boy, with numerous cups of tea, leads me back to this singular small world of comfort, heat and shadow.

I know the boy is too young to be left alone. His sister should be in school, not carrying live muntion for the Population Bomb. Yet it was they who'd rescued me! My objection to their abjection was a cultural projection, whereby I sought to gloss underdeveloped aspects of my own, such as a thirst to live.

It's understandable; these limits to a culture's self-awareness are crucial to its function as the blind spot is to the eye. When Doi wrote about his nation's shame, the Black Hole of Nanking, he did so in code, since naked facts might land him in gaol. Instead, he used the aphorism *The traveler discards his sense of shame* to explain the problem Japanese face while "traveling abroad in groups."

Recall: the underdeveloped individuality that results from immersion in *ame* leads to a scant sense of guilt; so Japanese rely instead on shame — the all-seeing Eye of the group — to keep them in line. Deprived of social context in Nanking, yet subject to group dynamics in their platoons, a terrible feedback took hold, as if guitars sat too close to amplifiers. That which began with standard rape and pillage metastasized into a fathomless hell as soldiers looked to each other for their sense of shame but saw only examples of their own most base proclivities — a downward spiral that soon had *cadres* raping everything that moved, or no longer could, then raping what was left with bayonets, then bayonetting slits in little girls so they could rape those too. Small wonder China saw Nanking as a war crime, while Japan could barely see it at all. For to grasp what truly happened they must face not just the facts, but the monstrous aspect of *amæ*, their sacred creed.

"HOT ... HOTTER ... OOH! ROBO-DAD! YOU'RE BOILING!"

CHAPTER LXI.

INNER TRUTH

Fatherhood — The Covenant — A pornographic theatre — Dhalgren again

CULTURES ALL HIDE INNER TRUTHS whose roots must reach down to hell, lest the entire structure topple; thus each would sooner judge another's sins than face its own. We find it strange the Emperor of Japan proudly traces his lineage back to the incestuous union of Amaterasu and her brother Nobukio; yet Christ can trace His own back to the incestuous union of Abraham with Sarah, who, as the Patriarch confesses in Genesis 20, is "the daughter of my father, though not of my mother". But such details won't help us glimpse the whole truth, for the problem is structural. As spake that ancient hillbilly Jesus, in the redacted Gospel of Thomas: "The Kingdom is spread out upon the earth, and men do not see it."

I certainly did not. Clearly the lost mountain kingdom I sought was the Land of Dad that lay before me; its ruined temple: Fatherhood. But I would sooner solve the world's problems than my own, which I had almost shuffled off the mortal coil to avoid.

Some men fear becoming their fathers: angry robots controlled by their emotions. My father was not such.

He sacrificed all for his family, but was of an age when the contract between men and women was clear: he provided safety while my mother provided children. This contract formed culture's backbone since before Noah wrested from God a Covenant: never again would He destroy mankind for partying. Indeed, Israel

means *contends with God*; and this refusal to accept the Orient's eternal round of creation and destruction has birthed our modern world. Later, when God vowed to destroy Sodom unless he found fifty good men therein, Abraham bargained Him down to ten.

But God is dead; all contracts are annulled, even the ancient one between the sexes. Why sacrifice all for naught? Be smithied into an iron ring that rolls emptily along through desert storms? And even were the contract firm, I would still be a gimbler. I might feign normalcy, but could never *be* that paradigm of such: the Family Man. I'd make a hollow mockery of fatherhood's sacred task.

Yet in Japan the most reverent conjugations, more polite even than those accorded to Emperors and infants, imply the adressee is only acting. When a man dies it is polite to tell his son, "I hear your father is playing dead" — for it implies the greater truth: we are but walking shadows, signifying nothing. Still, we might enjoy this hour upon the stage. I'd never *be* the Family Man; but I might play the part of Patriarch.

I'd start by setting up a trust fund for this little clan, who'd saved my life, and in whose company I deemed I'd learned something of my true nature. But I had learned nothing. By dawn the fire was down to ash, as were my dreams of patronage; and when the boy proudly presented his bill, I bargained him down. On reaching Pokara I found it roiled by *Tihar* — the Festival of Lights — so that every shop was shut, and chaos reigned. I still had enough hashish to sate the Grateful Dead, and only days until my flight, so took a seedy room above the station and set to incinerating it, but found the method wanting for speed, so crumbled ingots into coffee while delving through a dog-eared copy of *Dhalgren*, and at last made progress.

The novel's protagonist — the Kid — is every hero

simultaneously: he loses a sandal, like Theseus; he is an Outsider, like Beowulf. Yet he is also every villain, for if one starts to read the word Dhalgren in the middle instead of the beginning, it comes out Grendel. Whence came the extra *h*? I could not say; but on I trudged through half a thousand pages of tediously vivid detail, until I saw that this was the whole point: to embed the reader in time and space the way drawing does.

Halfway through the book the Kid is lost in a drug-fueled psychosexual labyrinth. I knew just how he felt. By day, my room transformed into an *ad hoc* pornographic theatre, where scores of fez'd young men sat cross-legged staring raptly up at British smut of Seventies vintage. To evade censure the film's action was framed by a dialog between a reverend and a doctor positing cases of perversion they'd observed "on the job". First, a Macintoshed pædophile lured a schoolgirl into his dented Bentley, then a Page Three-type came home from college and got jiggy with her little brother. Admixed with these monstrosities were tales of normal sex outside wedlock. The doctor told the cleric, "These women pose a dilemma for you and I: they love freely, yet are not criminal!" It was the least erotic film I'd ever seen. Compared to it, gimbling seemed good clean fun.

The night before the last bus left for Kathmandu I asked the manager to rouse me early; then smoked, drew, ate, smoked, slept, and woke to hear him brushing his teeth at a tap below my window. The bus was gone! What of my early wakeup call? "Oh, sir," he said, perplexed, "how could I wake you earlier than this? I've only just got up myself!" Then he flagged a rusted car that rattled past.

CHAPTER LXII

THE KID

*To Kathmandu by cab — A catastrophic
loss of blood — A near death / birth
experience — Hail, Cæsar!*

OUT JUMPED A KID OF FOURTEEN; his eight-year-old brother stood on the shotgun seat. I thrust a sheaf of worthless fiat at them and bade the elder drive to Kathmandu. It was Cow Day, and the streets were clogged with heifers wearing garlands. I told The Kid to warn me when we approached the next police checkpoint, then lit my pipe and slumped down on the back seat like a sack of rice. The radio played a tambla'd folk tune and we sang along with the one-word chorus: PO-LA! Clearly it's their top hit for it plays over and over and over but at least I'm connecting with the culture. I ask what PO-LA! means and the Kid says it's short for Polaroid™; then rain sets in to PO-LA!™ (la-de-*la*-de-la-*de*-la-de) PO-LA!™ (la-de-*la*-de-la-*de*-la-de) so I lie athwart the back seat watching jungle fronds lash past the window just like rollers in a car-wash as we race through villages knee-deep with muddy water because a humpback bridge along the river is clogged with vegetation forcing the Kid to skirt through a marketplace into a thicket of brown limbs that part to reveal a cow festooned with garlands which we skid into at top speed, and I watched dumbly through the side window as the door handle bites a fleshy chunk from its prominent ribs, then through the rear window as it falls forward on its knobby shanks with garlands swinging wet and yellow and black eyes filled with passive pain like all of Asia saying goodbye, then more hashish, then *"Polize! Polize!"* both boys shout down at me like Whac-A-Moles™ and I sit up to see the car has stopped in a cobbled courtyard full of army jeeps and trucks and tanks and the cab is blue with smoke through which I glimpse soldiers with smiles and berets and guns who rap the window and I think *I'm f__ked* until the Kid snatches his permit from the dash and climbs out the passenger window shouting that the driver's door is jammed and by the time the soldier lumbers to the shotgun side the canny lad runs round the front end of the car up to the checkpoint desk and stamps the permit himself so that the soldier scowls but by the time he's slouched back to the desk the Kid's already back inside the car (he must have practiced this) and off we go into along and down a jungle road between two lines of trees where I attempt to throw my dæmon hashish tangerine of dreams out the side window but my fingers won't obey my brain until I gaze at the sky and picture the child who's waiting up ahead and then the ochre chunk rattles in my caged fist like a seed pod — *you can do it!* — but I couldn't; then a random gust of wind takes it and I'm free, and good thing too, for at the next checkpoint soldiers alerted by the reek search trunk and ashtrays but find nothing they can bribe me over; and as the sun sets we screech up outside the Lhasa Hotel where the Manager stands behind the big front desk wearing my magic waistcoat. "Oh sir!"' he said, "I thought you were gone for good!"

The airport was a turmoil of construction, for the Concorde was scheduled to land there in a month. The Future had arrived. *Time* on the plane showed saffron'd monks hurling bricks at the flaming Lhasa police station. But all intelligence was swept aside by news the Dow had suffered its worst loss since 1929. As I approached the West Coast sun poured like molten glass on Vancouver's towers. By traveling east I was come home at last.

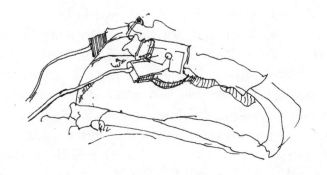

ULTRASOUND OF THE BABY

Safe in Victoria, Guinevere beamed at me, glad and big. We bought a car and found lodgings near Craigdarroch Castle. Crystal dropped by, and we resurrected that lost evening at the pub when she'd regaled us with tales of travel — but this time the shoe was on the other foot. Then in the lavatory I gushed a gallon of fleshy blood. Crystal drove me to the infirmary, where I swooned while silhouettes of doctors gesticulated like Balinese shadow puppets on the curtains 'round my bed. "He's been in Tibet," said One. "Ti-*bet?*" cried Two. "Shut down the ward!"

In isolation I learned amœbas had eaten through my rectum wall and tried to colonize my liver, which would mean certain death. But my body flushed the invaders out in a deluge of blood and shit. It was the most blood I'd ever seen, till Guinevere required Cæsarian sectioning. The baby bore up from the void fist-first; its head rose ruddy and oblate as the sun on the cover of *Dhalgren*. By this heroic act the doctors saved both mother and child — then tried to spirit the sprite away, but found I would not let go its tiny heel. For Guinevere, ere she succumbed to the æther, had made me swear I would not leave the infant for an instant: and I did not. Marvelous as these medicians were, I did not know them from Eve and Adam.

Hubbub ensued. I was hauled up before the Matron, who said, "We have work to do, looking after your wife and baby, and we'd like you to get out of the way." I saw her point, but was unswayed. She said, "Fine! Legally, I can't force you to leave. But I won't provide a bed." I said I'd sleep upon the floor. She said she would not provide bedding. I told her I could find such. She concluded archly, "Very well! But we *won't* feed you."

She saw my sacred purpose from an entirely different angle; so I apologized for the fuss and stepped outside, where my old nemesis Morwen came running towards me down the shiny corridor, her face flushed with relief and pride.

CHAPTER LXIII.

AFTER COMPLETION

Minimum wage in Tofino — Return to Chestermans Beach — A strange encounter — I foresee the Future

KEN, AFTER COMPLETION of a brief interview, rehired me at minimum wage in the pub kitchen, now redolent with what Freud called *unheimlich*, though Scots have a better word: uncanny. Even the grease marks were unchanged, as if I'd only stepped outside for a smoke — speaking of which, Dwayne was still gone. A month later he poked his nappy head through the hatch and said hulló. He was become Christian, and would attend seminary in the fall: "Gonna learn to save souls."

Three years later he lay face-down on the sward adjacent to Gary's theatre, in plastic sandals and a raincoat, one eye cast in abject horror across the grass. Ten years after that I saw him at a crosswalk in Victoria. "Shalom!" he beamed beatifically from between grey sidelocks; for he had converted to Judaism. Five years ago I met him coming through the graveyard at Christchurch Cathedral: round as a barrel, his white sidelocks knotted into dreads, eating chicken from a box and wearing many sweaters. Clearly he slept outdoors. We sat on a table-top tomb; ten minutes passed ere he recalled my name. Then like a man full fathoms five down a well he asked: "How's Guinevere?"

Each time we'd met I'd told him she and I had parted long ago, which made him sad, and to what end? This time I merely said, "She's good."

Which I held to be true, though it perplexed the Divorce Court secretary. "Separated sixteen years, and *now* you want a divorce?" We nodded, signed, and hugged. We were grown more akin to sister and

"HERE'S THE AD: 'LONE RANGER SEEKS PSYCHIC'.
DAMN! I TOLD THEM <u>SIDEKICK</u>."

brother, like Amaterasu and Nobukio; and looking back, I see the happy Land of Marriage as it truly was, but seldom is: lovely as sunset in the Himalaya, lost as youth; and say with Lord Asano of the *47 Ronin*:

> *Even more than cherry blossoms scattered by the breeze*
> *Memories of the passing spring bring unbearable regret.*

Why did we part ways?

Because the selfsame *wyrd* that drew us together across the globe now swept us apart. My path led into the forest, where I spent ten happy years homeschooling the Kid as she sprung up like bamboo alongside my artistic practice.

When her eyes opened I drew my first comic strip; when she learned to talk I performed my first stage monologue; when she learned to spell I wrote my first book; and when she took to the Internet I made my first viral, *Spiders on Drugs* — which strange tale is a book unto itself. Suffice to say, in cyberspace I am an Emperor, with untold millions in its currency of *clicks*.

Because gimbling is like a second language, and save for kissing, two tongues used simultanously yield confusion. So I followed a lonely road, which happily led through divers lush oases (and the occasional crowded truckstop). I am an Outsider, and as with *Wrestling Gaijin*, once I warmed to the role I felt closer to my true self.

And Outside was the place to be if one sought to live from art; for as with the American economy, whose mania for freedom has led round to the most unequal society since the Industrial Revolution, in cyberspace some artists are crowned Emperor while the rest become salarymen, who must exchange their content for a handful of *clicks*.

Meanwhile, Shanghai's SONY™ ad for the Future proved prophetic: that city grew so shiny that scientifiction films began to use it as a backdrop. Gorbachev freed Mathias Rust as a goodwill gesture, and used the incident to purge thousands of Red Army fossils, whence the Iron Curtain fell. Freed from gaol, Havel told the cameras a century of Marx had taught us Hegel. The Socialist Worker's Paradise collapsed into a black hole that can be seen from space, marked North Korea on charts.

Triumphant, the Future rolled on past the end of history and created a new *Cosmos,* whose pundit said of scientific law, "It's true whether you believe it or not." A wiser man, like Bohr, might have said *real* instead of *true.* There is a difference, which we call

When Tiananmen hit I burned Feng's card, lest I implicate him in my foreign devilry. In Germany, Mathias Rust fell for a nurse, who spurned him, so he stabbed her half to death. In Korea Kim died; Kim Il, on his deathbed, wrote to a cadre he'd purged and forced to eat grass in the gulags, "Forgive me. I was playing a role."

Triumphant, Everett's multiverse conquered physics without firing a single particle through a double slit, becoming orthodox by way of string theory, whose elements are too small for experiment, leading one pundit to say the theory, from which most physics doctorates now depend, "is not even wrong."

But that science should end in paradox is no shame, for this inexactitude has a name:

The Human Condition.

But I'm getting ahead of myself again.

CHAPTER LXIV.

BEFORE COMPLETION

*A cabin on Chestermans Beach —
Fatherhood — The Cheese Club — A
Serpent from the*

EVEN BEFORE COMPLETION of my first shift at the pub I vowed to escape the scourge of minimum wage, so took a position at the fish plant, cutting salmon. Now I was really down in the guts of life: tangled in time, steeped in blood, swamped by death — a killing machine! Winter bit my thumbs as I brailed salmon onto the dock; but watching gulls descend like workaday angels for the bloody eucharist, I felt an indestructible joy thrum in my chest: *I am!*

Yet though I'd twice the work, I'd thrice the steam-power. When Gary suggested I use my one day off to play myself on stage performing a monologue based on the tale you now hold in your hands, I said: "I'm in!"

And when the baby slept I drew an hour, much aided by the *frame* I had invented on my Asian sojourn (see p. 240); which like that ancient well in Lhasa, once primed, filled with cthonic content. The drawings were odd: few grasped their deep context, and for a spell I had but one supporter. By bluck he was the editor of the *Georgia Straight*, in whose august pages I soon became a weekly fixture.

THE CHEESE CLUB BY ANDREW STRUTHERS

"THE MOON ISN'T REALLY FOLLOWING US, KID —
THAT'S JUST AN OPTICAL ILLUSION."

Pay was slight; but a greater challenge than living from my art was living in a one-eyed world with ambidextrous vision. I'd realized at University, upon reading my brother's thesis on the brain, that I was one who did not distinguish left from right, which condition science calls *lateralized dysfunction*. As a result I was a political Outsider: for the Progressive plan seemed comfortable as a dentist chair, where all hope lay in analgesic and the Seven Wonders of the Ancient World were bound up in a single eighth: *I wonder where I put the TV remote?* Yet I was no kind of Conservative — unless it be the "embroiled" kind:

PILLAR OF COMMUNITY
EMROILED IN GIMBLING SCANDAL

But the modern world enfranchises only those who choose one or the other with unshakeable certainty. For me, fatherhood marked the end of such — for whether I walked along the beach or toiled at the fish plant, at any moment someone might rush up to tell me the child was gone, and my new world would come down in flame and ash.

What of it? By the laws of science there'd still be a trillion trillion worlds where both of us lived on, and others where I did not find my passport at Æroflot™; or was ejected from the Land of Wa for exposing my buttocks at Narita; or lie dead on Everest like Wilson (or was it Annapurna? *Damn!*) In some worlds Matthias Rust's flight sparked World War III; in some you are the writer and I the reader. This makes the future both predestined and unpredictable: to wit, I'd thought myself the last person to love fatherhood — but how was I to know my child would turn out to be such a little loser. "You're going to Julliard!" I shouted. "It's my dream!" And she threw a chair at me!

Therein I describe a contrafactual world — a place most natural to Celts such as the Scots or Welsh — which latter is surely the noblest of nations, and gave the world the great Sir Richard Burton (the actor, not the explorer) and the eponymous Sir George Everest, who first laid scientific eyes on the Mother Goddess of the World, Chomolongma.

SIR GEORGE EVEREST, WELSHMAN & HERO

Through Wales I came at last to my true country — the Land of Dad — and spent my first long summer there with that beloved Scotwelsh infant swaddled upon my back, walking along the waves to Henry's End. Such treks exacerbate my great uncertainty towards life, for in counterpoint to the fathomless beauty of

Chestermans, the Voice hums dark notes that unfold like drunken origami cranes and take flight in my mind:

As the small bundle on his back grew cold and
stiff he realized the child had perished . . .

Then I squeeze her snugglied toe until she stirs, aware this constitutes poor parenting, yet relieved the worst is yet to come. We've spent so many hours on this faraway beach we know every creature that lives on it, in it and above it.

But one sunny evening we come across a beast I've never seen before, and still cannot believe exists, even while staring at it: a nine foot snake with needle teeth, a long webbed fin and blue-green eyes translucent as Japanese glass floats, one already pecked away by gulls. "Behold!" I say to the wondering child upon my back: "A sea-serpent cast up from the

AUTHOR'S F____ BOOK™ PAGE

BY THE TIME I FINISHED working on this book my life was in ruins, and only stood by virtue of inertia, like those perpetually burning buildings in *Dhalgren*. For seven years I'd made my living by selling art: films, drawings and writing. But that triple stream of revenue ran suddenly dry; and though my YouTube channel had earned forty million clicks, they're not redeemable for CASH! The Internet is communalist by nature, and no matter what tolls are set the tides run over them to find the sea. There's no connection between dollar and widget, so monetizing is akin to growing lettuce in the desert, or democracy in Africa. That the West's best capitalist intentions have led 'round to this most socialistic of cultures is no surprise to Asia, who chalk up such ironies to the unseen hand of Tao; yet we are as a chimp spooked by its own reflection.

Bills piled up; rent went unpaid. For victuals, I painted a house in Fairfield. Such is the artist's life, and should be thus, for art and money are oil and water.

But this time I was not alone; around me, entire fields collapsed. An epochal shift was underway, as when the mighty Indus changed its course seven thousand years ago, consigning humanity's first great civilization to the dust.

Marx wrote that new technologies wreak upheaval in a culture's foundations, on which were built the superstructures of church and state — and the Internet has caused a shift in the Voice more profound than when Luther dismantled the confessional booth: the *vox publica* to which writers were once handmaids has through F___book™ become a *vox populi*. The need for books, and writers, is no more.

Stories are another matter; that matter will not pay the rent. To misuse Marvell:

> But at my back I always hear
> Rent's grim steamroller trundling near.

Yet to write, one must withdraw from such quotidian concerns; by which I mean I stopped answering my phone lest it be Visa™ demanding CASH! I did not have; then I ignored the mail, lest letters from the landlord distract me while I toiled; then I quitted F___book™ — or tried, for it's easier said than done.

The socialist network, which began with the millennialist joy of finding friends and relatives from days *lang syne*, as if we'd congregated on some faraway beach filled with sunny smiles and gnomic graphics, had become a virtual Panopticon: Jeremy Bentham's circular prison, whose single central guard can see into every cell. Bentham's master stroke was to render the guard invisible, for inmates who may or may not be observed, yet always feel they are, behave accordingly, and eschew mischief. But the Panopticon's true genius was capitalist in nature, for thanks to its structure a single guard could control an entire prison population.

Zuckerburg's master stroke was to make each of us both the central observer and the surrounding population, who may or may not be observed, yet always *feel* they are, and so behave accordingly, rendering heretofore private domains public. But F___book™'s true genius is post-capitalist, for it is built and maintained by We, the Inmates.

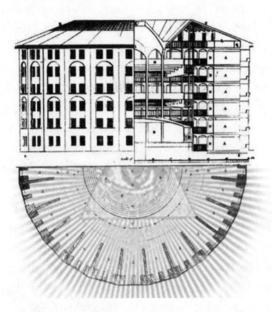

DESIGN FOR PANOPTICON / F——BOOK™

And such excellent inmates! I soon located the Guest House crew, or at least learned their divers fates. Erik, Victoria, Matt, Brian, Jocelyn, Trigg, Barry and myself were all become writers. What strange broom swept us into that same corner none can say. Barry edits a journal in some island paradise; Trigg is a diplomat; Ganden's *wyrd* involved an actual Goddess; Jack refused contact but left a comment calling me a c__t; Greg works for a Japanese shipping company; Kris has a little family in Sweden; Jocelyn has the same in London; Bill lives just across the strait in Washington; and Erik harbours a shameful secret which I shall now divulge — but suddenly he imposes upon me the fearsome *Shining Wizard*, so brutally that I must dine on mash for weeks!

Jeff lingered in Japan for years, in a rickety old house that leased its garden as a parking lot, with his girlfriend, her mother and her grandmother. One day her estranged father knocked on the door. Motivated by *amæ*, Jeff felt it might alarm the man to find a strange *gaijin* in his daughter's house, so hid under the stairs — then wondered if the man had a key, for if he entered now the scene were twice as strange. Jeff hid upstairs; then in the bedroom; then in the bedroom closet. By hapless *amæ* he'd painted himself into a corner.

And now th'entire population has done the same: In 1990 the economy collapsed; there followed a lost decade whence that vibrant culture withdrew from the world like Tolkien's elves, a process Doi foresaw back in the heyday Sixtes, when he wrote that as the matripatriarchal social structures that upheld the field of *amæ* collapsed in the wake of World War II the Japanese sense of shame in the eyes of the group would transform into a sense of fear. The result: a third of females under thirty are virgins, and two-thirds of males are *soushoku danshi* — "grass-eating men" — sexual herbivores who have no will to woo, yet are positively outgoing compared to their sibling *hikikomori* — "pulling inward" — shut-ins who commune by Internet alone, societal black holes in the final stage of *amæ* collapse who now number three million souls. Imagine the entire population of Wales incarcerated! But I digress.

In this Japan, whose population is set to halve in the next five decades, still heralds the Future, only now it's one we do not like. Our economy has collapsed, and only stands by virtue of inertia; our own lost decade is almost done, yet still there is no progress. The Internet blooms with strange communities such as MGTOW — Men Going Their Own Way — subscribed by fellows so disheartened by the contract between the sexes they're opting out *en masse*, choosing isolation over alimony. Conversely, gimblers, once so isolated, are now knit, but in two distinct groups: those who tighten the gimbling frame until it cracks, and those who hold frame-cracking to be sick and evil, and now the two camps shun each other more than the sexual orthodoxy once shunned them.

To counterbalance the Internet's proclivity for splitting into such clans, the unbreakable ring of F___book™ now binds us. Thus I found escape impossible, or at least impractical, for writing this book required much back-and-forth with the divers characters involved. I had enough worries without adding obstacle: I painted by day and wrote by night, and on top of this set out to finally finished *Dhalgren*.

On third attempt the novel seemed to be about an Outsider — the Kid — who comes to the city of Bellona, which has suffered some unknown cataclysm. His Outsider status is essential, for the same reason that Buddha, almost unkown in his native India, became the Light of Asia; and Marx, whose effigy was burned in Germany, is enshrined with Engels in Shanghai; and Christ, executed in the Holy Land, became the force that bound mediæval Europe: only an Outsider's eye can provide the missing element in a culture's vision.

But unlike Theseus or Beowulf, the Kid does not bring new life to Bellona: *he has come to to wound the autumnal city*, so that it might return to dust. He fails: the buildings burn on, without collapse.

This modern vision of hell was soon made manifest through the terrible news my sister telephoned with while Rolf and I worked on the first draft of this book: my father had been felled by a massive stroke, and spent the subsequent months demented and restrained, trying to fight his way out. Medical science worked miracles to stave off death, but was powerless to take a single step in its direction. He was suspended in collapse, as our New Covenant demands; for we are required by law to thwart our natural return to dust.

I won't dwell on detail; but it's sad to see one's captain shackled thus. On deadline day I sat not at my typewriter, but at my father's deathbed — which word was never used; rather this was *end-of-life* — while doctors told our family a botched catheter had given the invalid septicemia. My heart was glad: he was so hale he might have lingered, shackled and demented, two decades or more.

The doctors said he'd last a day; he lingered six. As was their creed, they stilled vast seas of pain, yet could not cause a single pinprick that might have sped his flight, so let the poor old fellow die of thirst while we watched. We never left his side, slept on the floor, and ate at the Tim Horton's™ in the lobby, whose sand-

wich board displayed a bold attempt by that old capitalist Voice to be heard still, for the smallest size of
coffee was marked

NOW UNAVAILABLE!

in happy font, as if the customers had won a prize. I
rode the elevator past the third floor, where my daughter had been born, to the sixth, where my father lay
dying, and thought of the ordeal ahead. But death,
like life, is never as one imagines it will be. A nurse
told me in the elevator he had *passed*.

He was the ring that bound us, from Scotland
through Africa to the New World; now we ringed him,
and wept. I laid my head on his chest and sobbed,
then rose before the warmth in him could fade and
saw I'd cried two dark patches on his blue simmet,
like twin black suns on a cotton sky. But I exited the
building along with three newborns, and through
tears reminded myself this was the winning hand, for
my father had Houdini'd his way out of that modern
hell. Returning home I found an eviction notice on
my door.

Now seemed an excellent time to visit my daughter,
who lives in a little cabin on Chestermans Beach. As
for the disaster of my life, who knows exactly what the
Future holds?

Non rebus, sed verbis.

Good luck!
Chinatown, Victoria
Fall 2014

COMMENTARY ON THE TEXT

PREFACE. *Daylight upon magic* — Bagehot.

1. My brother's thesis dealt with Sperry's experiments on the *corpus callosum*, a member that connects the hemispheres. One idea broached was that the left/right hemispheral split was a cultural projection. At that time it was thought the corpus connected the hemispheres; subsequent research indicates it also acts as a wall, allowing each hemisphere to inhibit activity in the other while it performs ithe tasks at which it excels.

3. Morwen taught me the technique of Transcendental Meditation™ but I did not stick with it, for drawing took me deeper and had the advantage of providing a living from the results. While those three kept the om fires burning I walked the family dog; for Maharishi taught their higher vibrations might injure the creature — which seemed odd, for of that clan the dog was most calm by far.

4. Benjamin.

6. Behold the mirror alphabet:

ABCDEFGHI JKLMNOPQRS TUVWXYZ
ZYXWVUTSRQPONMLKJ IHGFEDCBA

Certain short words (such as the biblical interjection LO!) are written forward in the regular alphabet to appear reversed in the mirror alphabet. There are a handful of three- and four-letter words, but no five-letter words, as the odds against such become near-infinite. Yet a six-letter word exists: WIZARD. This may be no coincidence, for the same characters who arranged the final spelling of that word also arranged the alphabet. Hence grammar and glamour stem from the selfsame root, as do spell and spelling.

Nietzsche was later bowdlerized by Jung into the F___book™ meme "For a tree's branches to reach heaven its roots must reach to hell." Jung attributes "Thus Spake Zarathrustra" in his footnotes; this vagueness has birthed a war on the Internet as to the quote's origins. One would need both the physical book *Aion* and a knowledge of both works to get to the root of the conflict; the Intenet is not known for such research.

7. The pub cooks were all male, the waitresses, female.

8. The arrangement of the hexagrams in the I Ching is arbitrary, as is the arrangement of this tale alongside them.

9. Technically speaking, Xeno was objecting to the idea that the world could be cut in half, by showing that the paradoxes that arose from postulating such exceed the paradoxes that result from postulating an underlying unity.

10. Lindstrom was recently implicated in an African gold mining scam.

11. I do not subscribe to the idea that quantum mechanics provides wiggle room for ghosts.

12. Nietzsche meant the supernatural God is dead.

13. Years later I jumped again; again, the jumpmaster felt obliged to say during training that "Women get hysterical" when they jump out of an aeroplane.

14. The house on Redfern was sold a week later. I had forgotten about the realtor's sign. Dismayed, I climbed the stairs to Bill's dark room and said, "You'll never guess what ha —" "They sold the house," he said. He had for months sat under his Hiroshima poster staring at the realtor's sign and thinking, any day now . . .

15. The fog headline is apocryphal — which is to say, true but not real.

16. All indications are that Hadrian's Wall was a massive vanity project. It should be noted that while the walls that define the West — Hadrian's, Antonine's, Berlin's — were barriers, the Great Wall that defines the East is also a road — *i.e.*, a connector as well as a barrier.

17. My Grandfather was a baker with a stay-at-home wife; somehow, in the impoverished past, he was able to own his own home.

18. After 2000 years of surviving the most brutal elements the denizens of St. Kilda were visited by a reporter from the *Lon-*

don Times. The public was so incensed that modern Britons lived in such savage conditions that the population was transplanted to the mainland, where within twenty years all had perished.

18A. The kilt as we know it did not exist at the time of Culloden. It was invented, along with all of Scotland's "national identity", by the writer Sir Walter Scott in the 19th Century. For decades the bureaucrats running Dounray disposed of spent fuel rods in a sandy pit and pocketed the cash they saved. The beach will be radioactive for a million years.

19. There is, of course, nothing funny about Hitler, except this joke: Two old Jews decide to kill Hitler. They wait outside the cafe where he eats lunch. Noon comes — no Hitler. Twelve-thirty — still no Hitler. At one o'clock the first old Jew turns to the second and says, "My God! I hope nothing's happened to him!"

21. I have no idea how much Nigel's tale diverges from reality.

23. The House of Fraser™ was founded in Glasgow. The company also owned Lewis's™, where I bought *Dhalgren*. It had recently been purchased by Mohamed Al-Fayed, the father of Dodi, who perished with Princess Diana.

24. No one thought to explain that Sainsbury's™ was a massive chain of department stores, believing this to be self-evident. This reminded me of certain jungle tribes that have no word for green, as everything is that shade.

25. The handlers were not on strike; they refused to load our plane because of the Hindawi Affair.

26. *The Book of Laughter and Forgetting.*

27. As with Nigel's tale, I do not know if my neighbour's daughter's friend's tale is true. But it captures how the West saw Russia at that time: unknown, magical and full of prison cells. Presently this part is played by North Korea.

30. A *gaijin* card is a small passport-like document that aliens must carry at all times; some Japanese of Korean descent have carried them for generations.

32. In Seiwadai an old cobbler came to our door with all her tools bundled upon her back and asked if we had footware she might mend. Guinevere found boots with worn-out heels. The cobbler glued and hammered them whole, apologized for her shoddy workmanship, and charged seventy-five dollars!

INTERFACE. Specifically, Wittgenstein abandoned the

"picture" theory of words he'd spent the first half of his life developing; his later work showed convincingly that words are context, and neccessarily vague. Therefore, all deep philosophical problems are linguistic misunderstandings that stem from this innate uncertainty — words are context.

33. Jung describes the importance of the sleep of reason to analysis in *Man And His Symbols*.

34. For literary examples of psychological incest between mothers and sons in Japan, see Murakami or anything by Mishima. It permeates the culture.

35. Thankyou/sorry.

36. In *Judgement at Nuremburg* the disgraced magistrate describes the effect of that small voice inside the radio that led them through the wilderness of the Weimar's social chaos and hyperinflation.

38. Hiro was dismayed by my attempt to split the bill because it indicated that this was nothing more to our relationship than a business deal.

39. (Bill's tale of sorry.)

40. Scientifically speaking, the only benefit derived from acupuncture (or religion) results from the placebo effect. My thinking was, if the placebo works, I want some.

41. Much has been made of Mao's use of *go* strategy during the Long March; however, this was a myth promulgated by his cadres to enhance his mystique. Mao barely knew the rules of go, and there is nothing in his campaign that resembles go strategy. Truman's post-war policy of containment, with Isreal and Okinawa sitting in *atari* around Asia, are much more indicative of that game; yet none accuse him of playing *go*.

42. The *Shining Wizard* entails smashing an opponent's face with one's knee.

43. The fascist demons of pre-war Japan are explored fully in Kobayashi's epic masterpiece *The Human Condition*.

44. The Orwellian trope that words control thought is called the Whorf Hypothesis. In World War II generals wrote their orders using up to 20,000 *kanji* (Japanese characters) but privates in the trenches could only read two thousand. Chaos ensued. Later the Japanese government reduced the number of *kanji* allowed in mass media from 20,000 down to exactly 1,945. If Whorf were correct one might have expected this to lobotomize the *vox publica*; it did not. But why choose that exact number? Is it

a reminder of their shame?

45. Deng Xiaoping was twice sent to the gulag for contradicting Mao, then reinstated. His famous critique of capitalism, "What does it matter if a cat is black or white, so long as it catches mice," is a delightful insight into the way the Tao transcends even the deepest ideology.

48. If the West has any right to intervene in Syria or Iraq, then China has twice as much to occupy Tibet.

49. The FREE TIBET joke was Al Anderson's

50. *Holy shit*: this is no metaphor; the Potala housed the shit of Dalai Lamas VII through XIII preserved in giant vats.

51. America — the true history of the Bomb.

52. Mao elided the horrors at Nanking because the troops there were mostly his political enemies, the Nationalists, whom he allowed the Japanese to brutalize. For something to fall completely into the "blind spot" there must be collusion of this kind. A sociological example would be the foxtrot around our disavowal of both male suffering and female agency.

53. Although I still BLEEVE in nothing, I find the similarity between my drawing of the irrational mind and temple paintings of the Lord of Death disquieting. But I'd need firmer proof of the supernatural before nail-bombing my opponents.

56. Travel in China was still proscribed; but one day in Kobe I was walking past the Chinese embassy and saw a line wrapped 'round the block. A paperwork error had led to the issuing of three hundred visas. Thus Guinevere and I were able to enter the country unchaperoned.

57. *Population Bomb*: Philippe Rekacewicz, UNEP/GRID–Arendal

57. The *hijra* were accorded legal status as a "third gender" in April 2013.

60. I am aware scientific orthodoxy sets the birth of civilization in the Fertile Crescent; I am writing this from the perspective of the Future, when cities along the dry bed of the ancient Indus, and especially those at the mouth, long submerged by the rising sea, come to light.

63. My cartoons were only censored once, in Berkeley, where without asking the editors redrew the Moon Following so that the cigarettes were gone and the child was restrained in a proper baby seat, its expression of measured distrust redacted as collateral damage.

64. Guinevere and myself cut all parental duties exactly in half; yet many would ask if I was "babysitting" my own daughter.

AUTHOR'S F __BOOK™ PAGE. One spring morning as I wrote, two suns rose. One was reflected in the glass of an adjacent tower. The illusion was perfectly convincing. From that moment, the trouble began.

COMMENTARY ON THE COMMENTARY

4. The dwarf is the religious impulse; and still exists, animating much of academia.

INTERFACE. Even the word *context* indicates this. Wittgenstein's work on language should have brought philosophical certainty to an end; it did not.

AUTHOR'S F __BOOK™ PAGE. In proofing *Dhalgren*, Delany discovered 900 or more errors; Rolf said, "We can beat that!"

SOURCES
IN ORDER OF DISCOVERY

Dhalgren, Samuel Delany — *Thus Spake Zarathustra*, Friedrich Nietzsche — *Love and Will*, Rollo May — *The Harmless People*, Elizabeth Thompson — *The Art of Loving*, Erich Fromm — *The Art of War*, Sun Tzu — *The Tao-te Ching*, Lao Tzu — *Drawing on the Right Side of the Brain*, Betty Edwards — *Creative Mythology; Masks of God; Atlas of Mythology; The Inner Reaches of Outer Space*, Joseph Campbell — *In All Her Names*, J. Campbell with Charles Muses — *The Decline of the West*, Oswald Spengler — *God and the New Physics*, Paul Davies — *What Is Life?* Erwin Schrödinger — *The Annotated Alice*, Martin Gardner — *A Dictionary of Word Origns*, Thomas Shipley — *Physics for Poets*, Robert March — *The Sorrow of the Lonely and The Burning of the Dancers*, Edward Schieffelin — *The Dancing Wu Li Masters*, Gary Zukav — *The Tao of Physics*, Fritjof Capra — *Swimming to Cambodia*, Spalding Gray — *Labyrinths*, Jorge Luis Borges — *The Fourth Dimension*, Rudy Rucker — *Jokes and Their Relation to the Unconscious; Moses and Monotheism*, Sigmund Freud — *Male and Female*, Margaret Mead — *Sex, Drugs, Violence & The Bible*, Chris Bennett — *Cows, Pigs, Wars and Witches*, Marvin Harris — *Gulliver's Travels; A Tale of a Tub*, Jonathon Swift — *The Anatomy of Dependence*, Takeo Doi — *The Magic Mountain*, Thomas Mann — *Tractatus Logico-Philosophicus; Philosophical Investigations*, Ludwig Wittgenstein — *The Parallax View*, Slavoj Žižek — *On the Concept of History; Art in the Age of Mechanical Reproduction*, Walter Benjamin — *The Origin of Consciousness in the Breakdown of the Bicameral Mind*, Julian Jaynes — *The Master and his Emissary*, Iain McGilchrist — *The Cleanest Race*, Brian Meyers — *Dhalgren*, Samuel Delany

OTHER BOOKS BY
ANDREW STRUTHERS

THE GREEN SHADOW

A hilarious illustrated account of life in the previously sleepy town of Tofino, during the heated controversy over the proposed logging of B.C.'s Clayoquot Sound. *The Green Shadow*, which was originally serialized in the *Georgia Straight*, won Struthers a National Magazine Award for Humours.

THE LAST VOYAGE
OF THE LOCH RYAN

Evicted from his Tofino pyramid, Andrew Struthers has the solution: buy an old fishing boat going cheap *via* the federal government's Mifflin Plan, and move onboard with his nine-year-old daughter Pasheabel. His perennial housing problems are solved — or are they? *The Last Voyage of the Loch Ryan* picks up where *The Green Shadow* left off, offering a account of small-town life in British Columbia. Packed to the gunwales with fascinating West Coast ship lore alongside affectionate accounts of the author's neighbours, it boasts at least one good laugh per page.

BREAD AND CIRCUITRY, *OR:* FIRST CHURCH OF CHRIST, FILMMAKER

This post-cyberpunk romp through the history of cinema, both film (1895–1995, R.I.P.) and digital (1995–2012, R.I.P.) is a first-hand account of how the author's short film *Spiders on Drugs* went viral, and the strange experience of going to bed poor and uknown, and waking up world-famous, yet mysteriously still poor.

THE MADNESS OF PRINCE GEORGE, *OR:* AMERICANFACE: A MEETING WITH THE UGLY SPIRIT

This comic *Bildungsroman* catalogs the mental upheaval of a lad cast from the small pond that is Scotland into the endless frozen or sandy vistas of Prince George BC in the mid 70s, culminating in the author's escape to Vancouver; his mental collapse following the emergence of his *doppelgänger* Americanface, which W.S. Burroughs called the Ugly Spirit; and finally, his repatriation to that little chunk of British paradise, Victoria.

ORM
AN ILLUSTRATED EPIC FANTASY

In the city of Atlas a guild of Scholars holds back the sea of superstition that surrounds on all sides. But is this the result of superstition? Or is there truth to the old belief, the Law of Distance: that the scientific method drops off the further one travels from Atlas. Polymath scholar Magus Finegal Kelly must find out, sent on his cracking aged knees to the far West, "where even the sun dies", to investigate rumours that the great sea serpent, Orm, has returned.

```
F t h r c k f d o j d k d k d j i h d b k y g y b l
h y r s g h g y f g b h g f d f h g b
y g g u y t d l b c g g k l k j h g f d c v b h
u y k h l i u g h j b h g l ; k h h w i o d i f h o i
i u o u g o u y g b j h g k h i k j h u h h j h k g
h t v r r v d v s u k l h g y f j b y b f k j h f b h n
h f d s q h g j p i i b h g f j g v j h j h g
y g g y t f b h g r b k j h g j g u o t w e j o k l k o f
j h g j u d d s e u g f o h y t s e w b t v v
b f s c b l j k h f b v c j n k c s x c , j n g j h g h g v
k u g b t b f j t h y r h y d f h g l j l j h j
j h g b h g f b r d b j d k d k d n e i c k g v k j h v k h b l j b
n y g n l i u g o y h y h c c k d n d n d h t h r t g i u y g j y
j g u h y g o u c e f g y g h y h g t i g l u h
j h y g u y g o y u g j v k j h d j i e n v k v j g v h g v g h v k g
k g l j l h l h f s h g x e a z d s a s z a z d z f
b l j k h f b b l j k h e e c i u e v c j n k c s x c ,
g j h b j h b j d g z x s r c d o f p e o e s d f g h j u y g h j
j g g i y n o n u n i y t d e i u f s - w ; s a s x e w g f b y t f b y
h g l h j g u y f y t u g v h e o e j c e o o d e g c j g v k g v m h g v
g r b k j h g j g u o d e i j e i c o s u 3 t w e j o k l k o f
j h g j u d d s e u g f k d e j i v c o o h y t s e w b t v v
k g l j l h l h f s h g x e a z d s a s z a z d z f
b l j k h f b b l j k h v d d l w p c d c j n k c s x c ,
g j h b j h b j d g z x s r e s d f s f o e k f p v g h j u y g h j
j g g i y n o n u n i y t d s x e w g f b y t f b y
g j h b j h b j d g z x s r e s d f g h j u y g h j
j g g i y n o n u n i y t d s x e w g f b y t f b y
h g l h j g u y f y t u g v h g c j g v k g v m h g v
g r b k j h g j g u o t w e j o k l k o f
j h g j u d d s e u g f o h y t s e w b t v v
k g l j l h l h f s h g x e a z d s a s z a z d z f
g j h b j h b j d g z x s r e s d f g h j u y g h j
j g g i y n o n u n i y t d s x e w g f b y t f b y
h g l h j g u y f y t u g v h g c j g v k g v m h g v
g r b k j h g j g u o t w e j o k l k o f
j h g j u d d s e u g f o h y t s e w b t v v
k g l j l h l h f s h g x e a z d s a s z a z d z f
b l j k h f b b l j k h v c j n k c s x c ,
g j h b j h b j d g z x s r e s d f g h j u y g h j
j g g i y n o n u n i y t d s x e w g f b y t f b y
h g l h j g u y f y t u g v h g c j g v k g v m h g v
g r b k j h g j g u o t w e j o k l k o f
j h g j u d d s e u g f o h y t s e w b t v v
k g l j l h l h f s h g x e a z d s a s z a z d z f
b l j k h f b b l j k h v c j n k c s x c ,
g j h b j h b j d g z x s r e s d f g h j u y g h j
j g g i y n o n u n i y t d s x e w g f b y t f b y
h g l h j g u y f y t u g v h g c j g v k g v m h g v
g r b k j h g j g u o t w e j o k l k o f
j h g j u d d s e u g f o h y t s e w b t v v
b f s c b l j k h f b v c j n k c s x
i u y g i u y g o u y h r t h t n g i u o u h
k j y f u t f g u y h y y h r f i t v h v
j h o f n z o t i m e t h y p y r a m i d s h j y g h g l u
k j h g l j l j l k j h l u y t d f v l g k j h v l i t
```